Dead Beat nation

What's Your Excuse?

Danny Lavergne

Copyright @ May 2010 Danny Lavergne- 2nd edition 11-2012.

Self Published by Danny Lavergne PO Box 270603, Littleton Colorado 80127-deadbeatnationexcuse@gmail.com

Cover Art by Kevin Zawacki at Elevation Creation, elevationcreation.com, kevin@elevationcreation.com

Printed in the great land of the United States of America.

DISCLAIMER

All stories about people and events in this book are fictional. Wink-Wink   But they are based on real life instances and some truly lame stories that happened to me. Seriously, could this really happen in America, people sacrificing homes for vacations, luxury items and lame excuses? Well yes. Although fictional, the information I am about to share with you is based on real life stories about people who apparently don't know jack about their own finances or just don't care.

Worse they may just be waiting for someone to bail them out, since that seems to be our culture now with everyone getting a trophy.

This book is far from perfect and I am sure there are grammatical errors and spelling errors. Just pen and ink them for me, would ya please.

This is my 2nd edition launch. I felt bad that some thought my language was a bit salty. So here you go folks, I cleaned up the language to appeal to a broader base. Instead of 110 sold, maybe 115 sold. Yippee! If you have an original, keep it!!

DEDICATION

This book is dedicated to my wife (editor and chief) who has put up with me during the past years of working in this industry, with the stress, anxiety and craziness, but to be honest it wasn't all bad. I let her make some calls (*you're welcome babe*) to folks to urge them to make their payments on time, so she got in on some of the fun. Come on, honey, tell the truth, it was hilarious!! Who knew we as a country could be this stupid? But again, how else do you figure some of these politicians get elected? (Sorry I had to fire you in the hallway, but seriously, were these calls making a difference?)

This is also dedicated to my good buddy who conned me into this business.

I am not done here! Pay attention.

This is also dedicated to my Mom and Dad who taught me to not be like the folks I deal with on a daily basis. Be responsible, pay your debts and buck up! What we deal with in life isn't always like smelling roses in a field. I learned from them that sometimes that person you are looking for to blame your misfortune on is amazingly staring right back at in you the bathroom mirror.

This is also dedicated to all my friends who will be surprised I could put some words together and navigate a computer and software. Surprise!

And last, I dedicate this book in all seriousness to the men and women of the Armed Services, who fight valiantly every day and risk their lives and some sadly give their lives so we can sit home, work, or play in a land that values freedom and liberty foremost above all. We should never forget what their blood has purchased for us and should honor them in our daily lives with a life that embraces that freedom with an understanding of the personal responsibility we have to ourselves and others as we go about our daily life.

ACCOLADES

"No s###, I didn't know you could write?"
Friend who wants to remain anonymous

"Seriously, a book, now that's funny."
Yet another one of those anonymous friends.

"A book? That's nice honey, go write a book"
Wife from dedication

"You might make millions, ha ha ha!! Maybe even make a lame movie about you"
Just another funny anonymous friend

"A book about what? Who would read that?"
Dumbass friend, actually more than one.

"That will be awesome!"
Designer paid for the artwork on the cover of the book.

"Good for you. Who helped you with spelling?"
Detective Smartass (Old HS Friend)
Investigations Division

"I can't wait til you write it. Is there good stuff on us? Make sure to get me a free signed copy"
Our Real Estate Attorneys, Servicer and Real Estate Agents- Cheap bums!

In the spirit of keeping the book PG-13 and removing some of my anger expressed in words, I have decided to remove the more aggressive words from this edition. Hopefully it will get a wider read based on that. Yea, right?

The first one had a chart equating strong words to meanings, but it is gone. Not to worry, I kept the original type on it.

FOREWORD

You hold it your hand... an immense undertaking of serious magnitude. An effort so daunting...ok, forget that description. This section just takes up some space and tells you that our economic system, as it stands, is in pretty bad shape. As a one-man lending-property management-shop I have had to learn the hard and exciting way about home loans and the rental business pain in this country during a time that this industry is constantly being pounded, discussed with no real answer and home lenders are ducking and dodging bullets from the media and government.

I wonder why anyone would lend money at 3-4% in a society where they protect the deadbeats by letting them stay in homes for 2-3-4 years without making a payment. Folks, I am not speaking of the hard working citizens trying to work with us or their bank, or anyone else to make it right. I am speaking of the Deadbeats and they know who they are.

We have the government slapping you in the face continually with the left hand telling you to lend money ("Come on, just do it!"); while the other hand is instructing the legal system to delay the inevitable, not allowing you as the lender to recoup your earnings or the assets pledge against these loans. Anyone see the math not coming out right here? See, that's what you get when you fill DC up with non-business people or people only wanting to be relected. They don't understand basic business or don't care.. The truth is that we and the borrowers are pulling on the same piece of rope and eventually one of us gets pulled past the line. Just hard reality. And the reality is not getting much better. Try and try to help or recover the asset and you keep running into roadblocks put in place by the legal system, which is our government rushing to protect their voting base it seems.

Ok, have fun reading. Some parts are more exciting than others, just like life, so be it.

Contents

Deadbeat Nation, What's Your Excuse?

INTRODUCTION

How do you start off discussing what is basically a mundane and boring business and one that tends to drive you absolutely nuts at the same time? Well, let's say it was a dark and gloomy night, or was it day? Ah, forget the fairy tale stuff. That is way too melodramatic for the insanity, stupidity, insanity, stupidity…sorry about the duplication there, but insanity and stupidity run rampant in this country. There is some emotion and heartbreak that I have to deal with, but that is with the hard working and decent folks sprinkled around our portfolio. I do wish there were more of them and I do wish there were a magic wand for those folks, but we have to protect ourselves and people get stung, not everyone comes out on top. Yes, some well-meaning hard working folks can end up on the wrong end of the stick, but life isn't perfect and you have to learn to move on, deal with it, and make sure to make decisions in the future that won't mimic ones you made previously that were mistakes.

Anyhow, this book is about the lunacy and flat out stupidity, ignorance and what I consider outright fraud in individuals that I have had to deal with at times. Ok, a few stories are about some people who are just plain amusing.

During my travels and time in the industry, I did find out where all the high school dropouts go to work. Yep, sure did. They sneak into the real estate market, the little urchins. Keep an eye out for them, they try to blend in with the smart ones, but they always end up showing their hand, greed or stupidity.

MOVING FORWARD…OR DOWNWARD?

I have spent hours sitting in a chair in my living room, on my deck and in my hot tub thinking in text language like OMGWTF! (Oh My God WTF) are these people thinking and doing and what do they expect from us? So it is really, OMGWTFATPTAWTFDTEFU! That is way too long so usually I just hang up the phone, lean back and say something I promised to not type in this book.

The business I am talking about is being a lender and/or a landlord on a batch of loans and properties around the United States. The genesis of all of this is hard money loans. The Wikipedia definition of hard money loans reads as follows:

*A **hard money loan** is a specific type of asset-based loan financing through which a borrower receives funds secured by the value of a parcel of real estate. Hard money loans are typically issued at much higher interest rates than conventional commercial or residential property loans, and are almost never issued by a commercial bank or other deposit institution. Hard money is similar to a bridge loan, which usually has similar criteria for lending as well as cost to the borrowers. The primary difference is that a bridge loan often refers to a commercial property or investment property that may be in transition and does not yet qualify for traditional financing, whereas hard money often refers to not only an asset-based loan with a high* *interest rate, but possibly a distressed financial situation, such as arrears on the existing mortgage, or where bankruptcy and foreclosure proceedings are occurring.*

Many hard money mortgages are made by private investors, generally in their local areas. Usually the credit score of the borrower is not important, as the loan is secured by the hard asset value of the collateral property. Typically, the biggest loan one can expect would be between 65% and 70% of the property value. That is, if the property is worth $100,000, the lender would advance $65,000–70,000 against it. This low LTV (loan to value) provides added security for the lender, in case the borrower does not pay and they have to foreclose on the property.

Making a short read of above, you can guess correctly I am not dealing with good credit score stories and wonderful borrowers all day long. It is more comparative to a recipe mixed with a life of stress and strain and a constant utterance of, *Oh my lord, what now!*

I get a real good mix of cultures and personalities to say the least. Some excellent folks (*few and far between*), some are struggling and many more just trying to use the system to their advantage in devious ways, and a boiling cauldron of lawyers working to beat the system in any way they can. I think many lawyers have a mission statement on the wall that reads as follows: *Stick it to them as much as you can and if you can't, well just screw them instead.* They take no sides really, just the side that is willing to cough up dough and then they cast you aside like a bad date when the well seemingly runs dry and doesn't put out.

Now for you attorneys that I like don't take this personal, you are a breath of fresh air for me and you know who you are, so just continue to read.

The results of this business are people crying foul about how they were being taken advantage of when they got their loan. Never mind that these same folks took considerable cash out with that same loan to live out vacation fantasies, or to just play or do something non practical like purchasing luxuries they don't need but want. It doesn't matter that these same folks signed their name many times to documents explaining new payments versus the old, and that they penned a personal letter explaining how they understand exactly what they are doing.

I don't even read these anymore, since I just roll my eyes and they don't play any role anymore in my decisions, and most certainly the courts could care less about these folks stating in writing they knew what they were doing. Seriously, all they seemed to care about was that they were getting more cash to do with as they please and they know that in this society, you can always claim ignorance and hold your hand out and fight to get your bucket under the government entitlement faucet. You have to push off a few greedy politicians to get to that faucet, but if you pushed hard enough you get there.

As my honest friends say occasionally, "I call bs!"

So how did I come to this business? In retrospect it was a result of boredom and the need to do something different, just like millions of other people in this great country. If I knew I would be listening to stories on a daily basis, some extremely lame, untrue excuses along with some sincere and sad accounts that would tear at the heart strings, I might have stuck with the gloomy day and boredom as a Government worker. Nah....this was too fun.

Alright, so how did this book come about and how did I get involved (roped into) in the loan business. Well...first off, be forewarned, if you want total political correctness, close the book and go do some new age chanting, while zooming around in your Prius, or trying to get your little solar panel to light the whole neighborhood while chanting or protesting whatever it is you protest.

My journey to the wonderful world of the loan industry truly started on September 11, 2001. I was in Atlanta, Georgia trying to leave town after the terrorist attack: the planes, the disaster and the eventual attack on civilized citizens of the world from those Muslim radical extremist. Oooh, can you say that still? *Muslim radicals*? This sent me on a journey to where I am now; dealing with the people I deal with today. On that day, I should have learned something about people and should not have been surprised at what (or who) I was dealing with on a daily basis working that small loan portfolio. I came to find out that there is a large mass of people in the U.S. that are not really that "quick" or aware of things in this country, whether it is the country they live in or the finances they deal with. It could be that these folks are just asleep at the wheel and they sleep walk through life to only occasionally stop to watch daytime TV talk shows or reality shows in between yawns and asking for breaks. These are the people that make some utterance that makes no sense, but you smile and your inner voice, says something like, "No kidding Sherlock" and you just smile on the outside and say thank you and move on to someone that can actually help you.

Anyhow, after the planes hit the towers, and the threat level across the U.S. was at its peak, I was determined to get out of Atlanta and get myself back home to Colorado pronto. Planes weren't flying, so renting a car was my only option. It was then that unbeknownst to me I was meeting future borrowers and renters. I started to find out more about people in this country by just trying to get the heck out of town. I have a somewhat funny and sad story about dealing with people that could have been one of our borrowers. OK, maybe not directly, but you will eventually get the point.

I went to the concierge's desk at my Atlanta hotel to ask for directions to the nearest rental car agency after they had told me they couldn't rent a car for me, like they normally handle. At that point, I just wanted to be pointed to the nearest car rental agency...*east, west, which way do I go?* Neither of the two hotel employees seemed to either understand me or seemed to know what east or west meant. I shrugged it off, marched out the building and finally found two rental car places a few blocks away. One had a line out the door that was ridiculously long, but the one across the street from it had no one in line. Odd, but what the heck, I would check out the empty one, although I was pretty sure there would be a valid reason that 50 people were in line at one place and no one in line at the other place. Right? No way they had cars if no one was in line at that time? So, I walked in, and sure enough, there were cars in the garage. What gives? I thought, so, I walked up and asked for a car. I was naturally asked where I wanted to go and I said, "Denver, Colorado and fast!" I tried to say this with a smile and some humor in hopes of improving my luck. Well, I was met with blank stares. They asked where Colorado was and what and where was Denver? OK, maybe they had never heard of Denver at a rental car place, but I really doubted it. COME ON! I kept telling them, "You know, Colorado, blue skies, skiing, and in the middle of the country?" Nope, they had no clue, I am not joking here, they really had no clue. Being a quick thinker and knowing that there really are ignorant people in this country who hung out on the school steps smoking weed and missed the whole school thing about the 50 states, I decided to possibly outwit them. With a quick conversation, I learned that they would only rent cars that could be returned to the point of origination for that vehicle, for those not understanding, this means from where they had come from (*light bulb goes on*). Ah, I thought, there is the reason for the long line outside the other place across the street. It took me a few seconds, but I thought, OK, these folks are pretty, let's say, unaware, lost, and stupid or just didn't care, so let's see where this goes. I sneak a look at the sheet of available cars on the counter in front of me and saw a car designated for Boston and I told the clerk, "there you go, it is right next to Boston." She was easily convinced, and happily rented me a large Buick that I cruised across the country at around 90-miles per hour that was going to take me to Denver, which as everyone knows, is right next to Boston. Was this my first encounter with a potential future borrower of our group? Yeah, this really happened, and this is the short version! Who cares, I got the car and whizzed back to Denver, which, again is... right next to Boston. Check your map, I am sure it is, or it was.

This experience gave me the great fortune to travel and visit many states on my way home. I stopped in various stores and had the opportunity to visit with many more future borrowers. It gave me something to talk about when I was talking with my wife on the phone during the trip and something to reflect on when I finally got home.

Anyhow, following this event, I moved around for a few years, worked for private industry and got bored, worked for the government and experienced what I perceived as fraud, people sleeping at their desks, folks telling me to slow down and all sorts of craziness that should be the basis for another book on government contracting and spending. Let's say, I was fairly frustrated with the Government so I moved on to a consulting firm.

About this time, a friend (*CEO of the one company I had wanted to work at for the rest of my career…prior to the Muslim extremist terrorists throwing a wrench into my life*) told me he was involved in a loan portfolio and he sure could use me, "only about ten to twenty hours a week." I fed him a friend of mine, which didn't work out, and he kept asking me to jump in and do the work. I had always been willing to provide minor Contract Management assistance to him on various business ventures, but nothing permanent because I had to work full time to earn a living and couldn't devote large amounts of time for assistance.

PS. Feel free to skip this part and get straight to the idiotic stories if you desire. You own the book

He is nothing if not persistent, and demanding. As I noted earlier, he was the CEO of a company I was working for during the time of the 9/11 attacks. I had known him and his family for over a decade at that time. The problem was there was not a way to work part time for him and still work at the consulting firm full time. I couldn't be available full time and then put in part time and feel good about it. He kept at it and finally I got the consulting firm to either let me go part time or fire me. They opted for part time but the loan portfolio turned out to be a full time gig. I would take my computer external drive to my now part time job. I would make my calls, work on e-mail, work loan problems, or whatever at the time since I had zippo to do and I tired of daily dart games, dice gambling and bs'ing daily, so I decided to do the loan portfolio full time while "working" this job. It was the most logical thing to do since I had already mastered computer games at the time.

Anyhow, the drive sucked and I wound up not doing anything but the loan work at my desk, and made no attempt to hide the fact after a while. You can only play so many games of FreeCell or Spider solitaire. I am not so proud to say that I played over 2000 games each: I kept the statistics. Plus there were some cool games on the computer; I played poker with the guys and had a six month run of darts in the office. Yep, we were slightly underworked but getting PAID for a full time job. Whoa, I a Government worker in private business?

A few years later, I'm working fifty to eighty hours per week, calls coming at all times of the day and night and on weekends, and I found myself truly tied to this business. My friend was kind enough to give me an incentive to keep me motivated, although on some days, I really felt like I could give a damn and got tired of the excuses that I had to listen too on a daily basis. Excuses that wear on you and depress you at times. Hard to work a job with no positive feedback on a daily basis.

Eventually the job got manageable and I got accustomed to the late night calls, maintenance issues on weekends, calls about dead people being pulled out of homes, homes shot up, amazing stuff found in houses and just the routine calls about people not paying rent or mortgage. You sort of get in a routine (*or do I mean rut?*) and become jaded to the constant barrage of weird stories, lies and emotional issues. Other times it just gets to you, emotionally draining. The honest sad stories were the toughest. There are sincere people who fell on hard times. The truth of the matter is, no matter the sincerity, the stress or money-management concerns, it shouldn't fall on our small group of families (*with our own hardship stories*) to support a financial asset like a home for someone, so we had to foreclose many of the times. Sympathy can only go so far. People should not continue to ask for one more chance over and over again but I can't blame them for trying I guess. There comes a time to cut your losses and move on. Dealing with taking someone's home is stressful, emotional and not an easy task, but I started to think I was doing these folks a favor at times. A home mortgage, insurance, taxes can be a huge burden to folks who just cannot afford it, and renting simply becomes a much better option. I spoke to every borrower who would listen about how to clean up personal credit, the total cost of owning a home, etc. We even paid for this support. The bottom line is that most of them didn't pay attention and that is where this book goes. It is the ones who will fail regardless of how many options and opportunities you provide.

How in the world would someone thousands of dollars in debt, owing years of taxes, with yet another year coming due and still not able to afford a mortgage which has been reduced to less than $1000 continue? The bottom-line was inevitable.

Anyhow, the rest of this book gives some funny insights and stories and some not so humorous insights and accounts into what I dealt with during my time as the one and only grunt working the portfolio. I was acting as the Vice President, Secretary, Accounts Receivable, Accounts Payable, Counselor, Grunt, Collections Agent, nice guy, the wonderful compassionate soul and the mean and ugly guy who would throw someone out of their home for being 6-48 months late on rent or mortgage payments. "You are a bad man, bad bad man." Ah, screw it! You name it and I wore that hat, and I was the only whipping boy for our small company. My friend would weigh in most weeks with plans to fix things and ideas to help people get to a better place. The trouble is reality, law and/or some regulation was working against us. I have to say I wouldn't have agreed to do this for anyone else. No better man than this guy. Dedicated and honest, like a hungry lion at a fresh lawyer, er, I mean jackal kill when it comes to protecting his friends' and families' investment.

Lastly, I have to say, we had some very good people and families in this loan pool and some great renters and not every one of them was a loon or lacking in common sense. Some of these folks were borrowers who found a way to improve their position, work with us, and eventually got a new loan or made the smart decision to sell or downsize rather than lose a home they truly could not afford.

Thinking with clear heads and avoiding the thinking that is guided by pure emotion is paramount. Those are the people for whom I take my hat off, the ones who will brush themselves off and get back up on the horse. The other folks want the horse washed for them, fed and rode while they sat on the porch drinking sangrias, diet cokes or smoking week and doing whatever! We did have folks who decided to take the option of giving the home to us through a deed and renting it back with a purchase option down the road when things improved. We have many in that situation now in late 2012 and pray they succeed along with changes in government and the economy helping to support the housing industry. I also must give kudos to the friends and family of some borrowers who stepped in to help family and friends. Those people were lucky to have someone intervene and help them navigate their difficulties.

But this book is about the other folks, who either just didn't have the acumen to handle their finances or purposely tried to beat the system and take what they could from us or the government, without a guilty thought or inkling of the repercussions. These folks ruin things for everyone else, and they never ever take responsibility for their actions.

Amazingly this description souldns like politicians. These people are the ones that Americans end up subsidizing through entitlement programs, stimulus funds and every other example of Government robbing Peter to pay Paul. Yes, redistribution of wealth. Just recently I received an email and I thought it was so applicable to housing and everything else we touch in this country. It reminded me of a recent episode in the Emergency Room where I could hear and see patients floating in around me as I waited with my father. You see people discussing their inability to pay who are indeed loaded up with hundreds if not thousands of dollars of tattoos, high end shoes, designer jeans, leather jackets, that we all know cost big bucks and expensive jewelry hanging from their necks, nose, ears, mouth, eyes and anywhere else you can stick one and yet they cannot pay any portion of their health care?

I have no clue if this is true story or who originated it, but we all have seen similar instances in our lives. Here is the email in full.

During my shift in the Emergency Room last night, I had the pleasure of evaluating a patient whose smile revealed an expensive shiny gold tooth, whose body was adorned with a wide assortment of elaborate and costly tattoos, who wore a very expensive brand of tennis shoes and who chatted on a new cellular telephone equipped with a popular R&B ringtone. While glancing over her patient chart, I happened to notice that her payer status was listed as "Medicaid"! During my examination of her, the patient informed me that she smokes more than one costly pack of cigarettes every day and somehow still has money to buy pretzels and beer. And, you and our Congress expect me to pay for this woman's health care?

I contend that our nation's "health care crisis" is not the result of a shortage of quality hospitals, doctors or nurses. Rather, it is the result of a "crisis of culture", a culture in which it is perfectly acceptable to spend money on luxuries and vices while refusing to take care of one's self or, heaven forbid, purchase health insurance. It is a culture based in the irresponsible credo that "I can do whatever I want to because someone else will always take care of me". Once you fix this 'culture crisis' <u>that rewards irresponsibility and dependency,</u> you'll be amazed at how quickly our nation's health care difficulties will disappear."

This is a summary of many industries I think, just like ours, where people balance and lose the battle of home versus the new H2 Hummer, home or vacation…you name it. People will spend money allocated for the home on vices and luxuries and go back to the well to ask for more or pity.

Enough already.

THE REAL STORY

Before I get into the real crazy individual stories about borrowers and renters, I think it is appropriate to give an overview of what I was really dealing with, and the constant strain and stress we felt from this investment. The loan portfolio had an average loan rate of 10.71 percent and an original Loan-to-value of 65 percent. This meant that the original lender lent $130,000 on a home appraised for $200,000. For example, as we progressed through the years, this number dropped in tandem with the economy and poor housing numbers that were being reported across the country. As for the interest rate, some would say this rate was ridiculous? Well, yeah, you are right; it should have been at least 12% since these folks didn't plan on paying in the first place. If we could go back in time and influence the original lender, I would say, no, you don't lend to these people and they wouldn't have bought the cars, the vacations, the drugs, or whatever they did with the cash out refinance. Further, the small businesses wouldn't be taking the heat in DC regarding these types of loans.

Are the rates high? Again, yes they are, more so in this day and age. But understand that risk/reward is a strict relationship and these loans were originated in 2007 when rates were closer to 7 and 8 %. There was a huge risk with these borrowers, so the reward has to be higher to entice lenders to loan people money to high risk borrowers. Low rates are for folks with great credit. What we are dealing with are folks that had a strong track record of poor financial decisions and dreadful payment history. Period! You don't reward these types of borrowers with easy and low cost money over and over. NEVER!! These are people that will leverage everything in their lives in hopes of getting more and more money to spend as they see fit and then they can and will whine and lie to you and ask the rest our families and the rest of America to foot the bill.

In every aspect of life and business, risk and reward are always related. Folks that lend to high risk individuals must get a higher rate of return to offset that perceived risk. That is the simple breakdown. If you are thinking 'no way, these are predatory rates,' just hang on. I don't believe in the term of predatory lending. But then again, I also think each person in this great country is dealt a brain and has the ability to discern what is or is not a good deal, and maybe you really don't need to put your house at risk for that new car, vacation, or whatever material item that you just cannot live without and want to purchase that is reasonably out of your financial reach. I am stunned more often than not by folks having a recently purchased brand new car while I am speaking to them over a period of years about being delinquent on their loan or their rent. How the heck do these folks get the credit to buy a brand new car? I am thinking, "This is ridiculous!" What are you doing making such a poor financial decision at a time where you cannot even afford the home you are living in? Maybe they just take a peek at Washington and our brave brilliant leaders, who spend more than they take in without a second thought. PEOPLE wake up! Try and use a little of that brain matter! This does not make economic sense. How about an older USED CAR?! ARE YOU HEARING ME! BUY A REASONABLY PRICED USED CAR IF YOU NEED A DIFFERENT VEHICLE!! Does it have to be the H1-2-3 Hummer, the top line Toyota, BMW, give me break? Do you really need to roll into your broken down driveway with big ol' shiny bling hanging from the rear view and 22's spinning up on your ride? Way to go people!. Make sure there is a sleeping bag in the back with a cup to relieve yourself into when you lose your home because of your spending habits and vices.

ME LIE? NEVER

Over the time of working this particular portfolio I got pretty jaded with people lying to me, not holding to their word, or just being dirty in their dealings. Recently, someone reminded me that we are dealing with a small slice of people and that most folks in this Country are hardworking and honest. I think this is true, but dealing with certain people for so long, you are not sure who you can trust. Eventually, it does tend to change your feelings toward your fellow man, and not in a good way.

There are obvious reasons people are not given ultra-low interest rates. I obviously cannot provide personal credit reports and detailed personal information, but you shake your head when you read these files. These are people who already had a history of defaulting on home loans, not paying car payments, credit cards, absolutely just horrendous. Did some of them have some bad luck or disasters that preceded this? No doubt some did, but the majority of what I have dealt with and speak about here is just about people making poor financial decisions or people knowingly gambling with other people's money. OPM's (*Other People's Money*). I use that term a lot lately to describe certain individuals who want to legislate through the political process to give themselves OPM.

It is my firm belief that you cannot mandate that individuals in private firms extend loans with high risk at low rates, or even mandate that they provide them a loan at all. The government is in the business of welfare, not private industry. Personally, I can say I would never have extended these folks a loan based on their credit history or financial position, but we inherited this thing and did the best we could with the hand we were dealt.

The upside, if there is an upside, is with the high loan-to-value, which means that a home with a value of $200K on the open market would have a $120K loan against it. This leaves a perceived $80K in equity, so it would be a good loan-to-value asset and maybe a reasonable decision to loan money against it. We were dealing with people with predominately bad credit, but who had some good equity in the property. Or so we thought. With the downturn in the housing market, many of these homes lost all the equity and were upside-down in the loan to value equation. Simply, this means the home was worth less on the open market that than what was owed on the loan. This is not a good situation for the borrower; or for us as the holder of the loan. But it didn't mean we had any obligation to reduce the principle amount as so many advocates in the government and media cried for lenders to do. My opinion is that neither government officials nor media talking heads know jack about business from the ground floor level, so clam up folks. As it was, our group routinely reduced payments for 12 to 24 months so borrowers could play catch-up, but even this was not good enough and in retrospect I realize people didn't use this time or reduction to shore up their finances one bit. So much for trying to help.

Nothing would fry me more than seeing public officials in their high end shoes and suits on TV, after taking one of their many vacations, and knowing they have money and pensions for life, asking our family group to reduce principal on a loan through a legislated policy giving judges the right to reduce principle values. (Anyone see a description of a politician in there?) You give up your jets, golf outings, pensions, cash and private dinners first!

A LOAN, NOT A GIFT

All the loans I dealt with were refinances. Borrowers took out considerable cash and then proceeded to default on their new mortgage. Many didn't make payment 1, yes, payment one and it took over 3 years on most of these to get the asset back, damaged and the worse for wear, but they knew how to work the system and cry to the courts.

Now, surely some did it for necessary reasons. Loss of job, medical issues, etc. Most did not. When you hear the stories at first you are taken off guard and have sympathy, but then you dig into the file, read the credit reports and see that this was long term and many were on a 1st or 2nd foreclosure bailout. So this is what I saw. People taking out $15K to over $200K+ and spend it on luxuries, trips, cleaning up prior years expenditures for fun and then they tell us they are not able to afford the mortgage payment. They take out thousands to renovate a home and, low and behold, not one upgrade had taken place! Give me a break people. Lie to your friends or your mother, not me.

With the downturn in the economy hitting hard in 2009 through 2012 and still going backward at full steam ahead, we couldn't get new money like everyone else, so the best we could do at times would be ask for the deed to the property and rent it back. Actually, owning the asset put us in a better position to secure new funding as opposed to just holding a nonperforming mortgage and the note.

There was always a common thread with most borrowers. They did not know how to manage their money and lived in a society that encouraged them to acquire everything they wanted. I remember during the 2008 Presidential election with all this exuberance and the 'hope and change, and Kumbaya feelings floating around in carbonated bubbles, there was a warm glow inside of everyone, right? I would get calls from people looking for more Government help and noticing how our payments were starting to come up a bit short. I actually, got a call from folks asking if I had some of that "Obama money." What?! Yep, you saw the internet stories about people thinking the new administration would pay their mortgage. I always thought it was a joke, but I am here to tell you, those people did exist; they lived and breathed among us, and they were our borrowers. How else to explain payments falling off the map as soon as he got elected? Sad day in America for all of us when you know people have got to the point where they think the government is going to buy them a house. How did they get to this point thinking this was possible?

And, no, this had nothing to do with race, sex or religion. We had a good mix of every culture from this Country, and every color and sex was represented in our loan portfolio. It had more to do with people not understanding economics, their finances, and the world around them. They understood only that they expected something to be given to them, it was their time, and they were owe it! The worst part is that it seems government officials are always on TV supporting these folks in their irresponsibility. unreal!

PLEASE BE COMPASSIONATE!

As I have noted, it was overwhelming to learn everyone's story, talk to them about finances, listen to their woes and develop not only a relationship with the borrower, but a plan to keep revenue coming in the door for our group. I was a virgin in this business at this point and wanted to believe each story, although I had been warned to not fall for all the sob stories. Oh yeah, they warned my sorry self to not believe folks. My buddy looked me straight in the eye and warned me, but I wanted to do some good, change the world, give away the farm, and convert to liberalism…whoa, what am I saying? Ok, I strayed a bit there.

So my friend might seem to be a little impersonal and not very compassionate about the borrowers, but the truth is, some people definitely had the sob story down pat, and it took me some time to distance myself and think through these things purely with a business mind set. I always wanted to believe in these people, but it got harder and harder as we moved down the timeline. With the experience of dealing with an individual, you begin to piece together all the hard luck stories over time and you see a pattern. Anything and everything that happened in their life, if it truly happened, it was used as an excuse for asking for financial forgiveness. At times, we would put someone in front of the house, or at the door, and see things like a new car they recently purchased, and at the same time they are hitting us up for compassion to help them financially. Situations like this helped me harden myself against the sad stories. One thing I have learned about Americans is that many will give up their home before they give up their new car. No kidding. It is repetitive in this book, but Americans rate themselves by cars they own or are seen in and they truly seem to value their cars more than any other asset in their lives. Actually, we had one borrower turned renter who lived 2 blocks from her job. She could ride a bike to work and not break a sweat, but probably couldn't figure out how to chrome it all out and put a banging CD and DVD in it. Her story? She lost her home as a borrower and home as a renter but purchased and kept her car during this whole process. More to follow on her situation later.

DEPRESSING

This business tended to depress me more than anything after daily calls and operations. How do you tell people nicely that their excuses for not making a payment are all worthless and there is no magic wand to make everything better? Worse yet is someone truly in need and we couldn't take the financial hit to help them. Those tore at your heart, but I had to make a choice at times. Us or them. Just the way it is folks.

Again, I interject that we had some who knew exactly what the game was, and felt responsible for their situation, and were fighting to make it right. Those folks were the ones I tried to give every break I could. The ones you really place your faith in and wish for the best. We just didn't have infinite resources to help them. Just a few years and then the inevitable would happen and we would talk deed-in-lieu (more about this later in a discussion of options), foreclosure and/or sale of the property. Too many could have and should have sold and didn't. When facing the prospect of losing your home, people often do not think logically and they keep the asset beyond the point of no return. Can you blame them? Probably not really.

Some folks were adamant about not paying and yet still wanting to keep their home. They had been bailed out before and not paid, so they might be thinking, "what's the big deal, someone will save my home if I make enough noise." When I was asked about where some government money was to pay their mortgage, I said, "What?" to one request and they hesitated and said, "Obama has money out there for homes." I replied, "Any money he has isn't his, its mine, my son's, my neighbors'." They then said that they guessed he really didn't pull it out of his own wallet, but they wanted some. That call disgusted me, to be honest. It was done in such a non chalant tone of expectation on their part. No interest in changing their lives to make things right. None at all.

I think Government assistance is good for those busting their butt and who need temporary help, but not for those who make a life out of Government assistance. Too many people expecting a flood of entitlement dollars, stimulus and bailout dollars where they consider it a permanent subsidy or worse yet a right! Boy, were they wrong and mislead. Sorry, went off-track for a bit...this is a different book on personal responsibility.

Credit scores were atrocious with our borrowers. We had many borrowers who paid more in total costs for one car in their driveway than they did for their mortgage. Who leases cars for $600-$700 per month with $200-$300 per month for insurance on top of that when they cannot afford an $850 monthly mortgage? Americans do it seems.

How insane is the fact that people have higher car payment and expenses than home mortgage and rental payments. My dad used to say, "You can sleep in a car, but you can't drive a house!" He's right on that count and I would laugh! That must be what these people figure. Worst case they can sleep in the high end car and shower at the YMCA.

FIRST CLUE TO RUN!

My buddy related a story to me prior to joining the company about a lady who wanted a break on her mortgage. He asked to see her finances and found that, yep, here it comes; she was spending more on one car than her mortgage. I know this is a constant thread so far but bear with me. Cars over homes! He then suggested to her that she sell her car and get something reasonable. This didn't go over well, something about her yelling "@&#^ you!" at him over the phone. I guess it's that universal code. Never ever mess with someone's car, the house yes, but not the car. It is apparently how some people define themselves. How dare we suggest that you rid yourself of high-cost vehicle debt? We just don't think folks, sorry about that. Go on with your bad self in that high-end ride as you pull into your weekly rental at the local run down motel.

Some borrowers think we should take more risk and reduce their payments, which we did for some. If they think they have a right to keep their home with little to no cost on their behalf, they are being misled. Heaven forbid they have to, give up nights out eating or give up putting those 22's on their rides, noooooo!!!! Their belief is that we needed to give them their homes for free or forgive them time after time for missed monthly payments. That got tiresome and very expensive for us over time. It just seems so odd that people would prize their car over a home for them and their children. Just amazing is all.

I always made a point to tell people of all the options besides foreclosure that were available to them, including selling their homes before they lose them to us and we pocket their equity, if any equity was indeed there. Some people did just walk away from equity in their homes. Were they ignorant, lazy, and frustrated? I don't know, but they were certainly misinformed. SELL YOUR HOME if you cannot afford it and do have some equity. Please, where possible, sell and get out from under it and rebuild your life. Why fight and fight when the inevitable is going to happen. Take your equity, no matter how small and get out. Now, some people, after paying an agent the six (6) percent fee had nothing left and just decided it wasn't worth it. But check your list of options and don't leave money on the table, ever.

The good thing about this downturn is it culled the pack of mortgage brokers and ran the bad ones out of business. I sure hope so anyway. Some good ones struggle to stay alive, but you learn to deal with the hand you are dealt.

YOU HAVE A CHOICE!

Here are some of the options I was able to provide borrowers. Usually I tried to email borrowers a few of the alternatives to get things moving and put the thoughts and ideas on their plate and in their minds early. This is how I saw it.

#1 Reinstate your loan and catch up. (*Most couldn't.*)

#2 Refinance your home on the open market. (*Again, most had ruined their credit at this point.*)

#3 Sell your home and pay off the debt. (*Limited success*)

#4 Turn over the deed to us for cash, avoid foreclosure and find alternative housing. (*Became more attractive to borrowers as we moved forward*)

#5 Turn over the deed, avoiding foreclosure, and rent the property back from us with a lease purchase option (deed-in-lieu). With this option, you then have a chance, although slim, of owning the home again in a few years or more. For trustworthy people that had a history of working with us, we could extend to three to five years. At times we even paid off liens for them. (The best option in my mind) (*Currently #1 option with borrowers*)

#6   Non-payment. This is the one most often taken by our borrowers. It is so much fun. Here is how it plays out. You don't pay and force us to foreclose; then you express surprise that you had no clue you were not making payments or didn't realize the house would be foreclosed on after not speaking to us for years. All the while ignoring phones calls, letters and even emails, you then call to beg forgiveness right before the foreclosure sale and are amazed when I decline to cancel the sale. (*This never changes and is still happening*)

#7   Purposeful non-payment and/or Bankruptcy. This was a frequent flyer also for our borrowers with the help of our nation's finest attorneys. Start simple by not making your mortgage payment; file bankruptcy, fight the foreclosure with your local greedy *(in my opinion)* attorney who is advertising on local highway billboards, and claim it isn't your fault. Go through the steps of expressing anger at your lender, pay your attorney fees equal to the mortgage payment, or even more to delay the foreclosure, and fight us tooth and nail, and then on the eve of the sale date or soon thereafter, beg and plead for another break, telling us the attorney gave you bad advice and again ask me to cancel the sale and express disdain when I don't.

Foreclosure. *Um, nope. Not going to happen to me!* Are you in shock thus far?

Put the book down and cry, go ahead, get it out.

You feel better now?

Yes, we actually foreclose on people and try and get the home back that was refinanced with our money. Let me restate that. This is our money! Not yours, not the Governments', OUR MONEY. Quit trying to take it from us. Why do so many Americans feel like they need OPM!

So you say you don't like any of the previous options. How about just stating you were trapped and had no clue you would have to make payments on a loan, a loan that gave you cash to spend seemingly as you saw fit, or you can claim ignorance at the amount, although each loan file had a minimum of five to ten documents and more that you signed with the new payment in **BOLD BLACK** ink accompanied by a letter you were required to provide saying your mortgage amount went from A to Z and you could afford it.

Oh, I forgot the really good option:

    #8   You don't like 1-7, then go ahead and destroy the house in foreclosure. Rip out pipes, break what you can, just because you are a lazy irresponsible person angry at the world and you think you should get a free home and wildly cry about the establishment and big business killing you. Why not, the media and politicians are all under a daze and screaming the same mantra. Down with Corporations! Down with free enterprise! Destroy the small business!

For that I say one thing: These people are nothing but criminal.

IGNORANCE

Just to make a point about what people know about their loan value and what their new payment would be, I present a copy of what is usually found in each loan portfolio: (1) A good faith estimate showing the anticipated payment (2) the borrower's note showing the payment; (3) 1003 showing payment; and (4) a note from the borrower understanding their payment.

I then get chewed out because someone supposedly fooled them and they had no idea that their payment would be that number, or they claim they never signed the documents and someone forged their names (probably the advice of counsel for this). Again, this is where I just shake my head.

Here is a random example of the notes in the loan file, most are handwritten, but I am avoiding those for personal reasons and of course because these are fictional stories...right? This is very indicative of the letters you would find in a loan file. This fictional borrower is actually one making a great effort to make things right.

May 31, 2007

Reference: Refinance / Debt Consolidation

To Whom It May Concern:

New loan
6/8/07
and the process continue

In the spring of 2005 we became behind on our mortgage payments due to my boyfriend, ███████ was severely injured at work and it took several weeks for the workman's comp check to begin. The pay shortage (due to no overtime being received) along with various medical bills did not allow us to keep up with our monthly bills. I had to reduce my hours at work so I could attend to his medical need. He has since recovered.

This new will consolidate our current 1st, 2nd and 3rd mortgage as well as payoff our credit cards, plus provide us with a little bit of cash to do some things around the house.

The total monthly payment of our 3 existing mortgages was $906 plus all other monthly debts — credit cards, homeowners insurance, etc. totaled $1375 approximately. The new monthly payment of $1049 with taxes and insurance included and all our other debt paid off will allow us a comfort level we have not had in some time.

We appreciate everyone's help.

Thank you

LOAN NO: ___

If someone picks up a mortgage note, you can read the note and it tells you the rate and the monthly payment amount. People tend to have 2nd mortgages on the property to eat up the rest of the equity. They just want more and more money. Money that turns out to not be there and the spiraling disasters are underway.

The point is this, there are many places in a loan file that each person reviews, or should have, and can see the rate, the monthly amount and any specifics on the loan. The truth is they care about one thing, that almighty check they get handed when the deal is done, that free money, the cash to spend.

Federal Truth-In-Lending Disclosure Statement

Lender/Broker: Premier Finance, Inc	Loan Number: EM006831	Date Prepared: 05/03/2007
Borrower(s): Leah Schilero	Property Address: 411 West Ritner Street	
	Philadelphia, PA 19148	

[X] Initial Disclosure estimated at time of application.   [ ] Final Disclosure based on contract terms.

ANNUAL PERCENTAGE RATE	FINANCE CHARGE	Amount Financed	Total of Payments
The cost of your credit as a yearly rate	The dollar amount the credit will cost you, assuming the annual percentage rate does not change	The amount of credit provided to you or on your behalf as of loan closing	The amount you will have paid after you have made all payments as scheduled assuming the annual percentage rate does not change
E	E	E	E
11.513 %	$ 251,729.95	$ 98,000.38	$ 349,730.33

Your Payment Schedule Will Be:

Number of Payments	Amount of Payments	Monthly Payments Are Due Beginning	Number of Payments	Amount of Payments	Monthly Payments Are Due Beginning
359	971.45	08/01/2007			
1	979.78	07/01/2037			

Escrow not included

TOTAL ESTIMATED FUNDS NEEDED TO CLOSE			TOTAL ESTIMATED MONTHLY PAYMENT	
Purchase Price/Payoff (+)	93,210.58	New First Mortgage(-)	Principal & Interest	971.46
Loan Amount(-)	106,200.00	Sub Financing(-)	Other Financing (P & I)	
Est. Closing Costs (+)	7,936.00	New 2nd Mtg Closing Costs(+)	Hazard Insurance	62.92
Est. Prepaid Items/Reserves (+)	458.26		Real Estate Taxes	50.67
Amount Paid by Seller (-)	0.00		Mortgage Insurance	
			Homeowner Assn. Dues	
			Other	
Total Est. Funds to you			Total Monthly Payment	1,085.05
		4,595.16		

[✓] This Good Faith Estimate is being provided by Premier Finance, Inc, a mortgage broker and no lender has been obtained. These estimates are provided pursuant to the Real Estate Settlement Procedures Act of 1974, as amended (RESPA). Additional information can be found in the HUD Special Information Booklet, which is to be provided to you by your mortgage broker or lender, if your application is to purchase residential real property and the lender will take a first lien on the property. The undersigned acknowledges receipt of the booklet "Settlement Costs" and if applicable the Consumer Handbook on ARM Mortgages.

BAD DAY IN PENNSYLVANIA

Some days with borrowers are worse than others and emotionally, these days just wear me out. I try and harden myself against the pitiful stories, the down on your luck issues, but this is not easy. They can just be so sad, heart wrenching and overwhelming.

Case in point: Late June of 2010, in the matter of a few days I was dealing with three people down on their luck.

I'll relay this story of one borrower who had stated he held a job position in the towers of 9/11 and after that day had to deal with not only losing a job, but losing close friends. He had finally filed bankruptcy. We had talked a few times about his situation, his job, his loan, etc. He sounded so sincere in his problems. I was pulled in and rode along for a while with his emotion. I learned my lesson though.

We gave him a break on his mortgage without much success from him buying into our helping him so eventually we had to file to remove the house from the bankruptcy after almost two years. We just weren't getting any money. It bothered me that this was a man who, although he had what seemed like many bad breaks in life, was still positive about life and understood our position. He called me to say he was sending his son off to Iraq/Afghanistan and on the verge of losing his home. He called me discuss a deed-in-lieu situation and we proceeded to execute one with an option to repurchase. The concern for both of us was his son having a home to return too, if indeed in retrospect he actually had a son serving in the Army (remember, I said I had become a little jaded).

Although this is a business, we try and do what we can to help our borrowers without hurting ourselves too heavily financially. Eventually, he turned the deed over and we wrote the lease option. The downside was that after only one monthly payment, he disappeared from the radar screen. This one bothered me since we both agreed to this deal and he was adamant about making this work. As I wrote this he was more than four months down and we had to have him evicted. The guy never made good on the deal. I paid some liens, too much in taxes, you name it. I allowed myself to get used by a user. Somewhere our politicians are screaming for us to help out on media shows without understanding the truth at this level. I continue to extend a hand and continue to get folks trying to bite it off. Just not worth it anymore.

Although I did file for eviction, I flew to PA in September of 2010 and checked out the house and to knock on the door. There was sadly no one home. The neighbor said she hadn't seen him in a while. Hmm? Once he got the eviction letter he blew up my phone. He told me his wife was sick and all sorts of other crap excuses. At this time I was starting to question his stories and honesty. He never returned calls or letters during the final weeks of our relationship. Even if his wife was really sick, you don't ignore calls and rent payments for months on end when facing eviction. But, I was indeed pulled in on this one and I worked out yet another a deal for him to deliver 2 months certified funds (his personal checks bounced) and we would work to keep him in the house. Why? I don't know, we still thought people were honest. How ignorant could I be in trusting people. I wanted to be right!!

In this case I wanted the check delivered to the Property Manager but he said something about his tires on his truck being bad. Oh man, that was a lame excuse! He couldn't drop off the check because he thought his tires were too worn? Good one? Stupid, but a good one! This guy was going deep into the barrel baby.

Was I being led on or what? I would hate to think I am being used because we want to respect his son's service to this Country and have a home there on his return, but I started to think I am being played and it bothers me. The end result at this point is that he made yet another commitment to provide certified funds but never came through on his end, yet again, so the direction was to evict and sell this asset. We ended up paying his back taxes. Over $9,000 to the city and state, as well as cleaning the place up to a tune of $5,000 and never saw him again. You can only go so far to help folks. What was odd about this one is that the borrower bragged to me at times that he made bonuses "back in the day" that exceeded six figures. If this was true, then why the defaulted mortgage? Lack of self-control, crazy or was this just stupid? You make bonuses that exceed the loan on your home and you end up kicked out? Guess he never thought of paying off the loan with these large bonuses, too many things to buy and have fun with. House, who needs a house!

This was my third and final time I allowed people to sell me an excuse due to military service. I was burned bad twice by two previous ex-military members. I got suckered. As an ex-military man, I have compassion and the utmost respect for those who serve. Those who choose to use their military service or lie about military service to purposefully avoid responsibility actually disgust me and dishonor those who do serve proudly and live their lives with responsibility and respect for others.

WHO PAYS THE RENT?

Same day that I got the screws put to me from the PA guy, I end up speaking with another borrower with whom I had already executed a deed-in-lieu, and had also paid off her lien on the property. I did all this after wearing thin trying to work with the borrower on the mortgage. Just couldn't make it happen. Didn't matter how much it was, it was always too much. Her husband was a drunk, (*Her statement*) her mother died twice (I don't make this up, and keep notes here folks), her aunt died, and probably all in the Caribbean so they could fly there (which they did). People dying around them left and right and they had to be there and pay for everything. Yeah, right, I believe it.

So, eventually it was obvious they couldn't pay anything, even with a full time job, so they agreed to just give me the deed. I decide to drop another $5K to pay off a lien, I'm just a nice guy, and then we executed a rent agreement that was about half of her old mortgage payment and the second combined. I also gave them a caveat to purchase the home back at what they owed us. Who does that? No one, but we do, since we are nice guys. Suckers!

She was not an escrow account and paid their taxes and insurance separately, so this meant we paid the taxes and insurance now, resulting in a large reduction in monthly living costs. Right out of the chute she had problems paying her rent, and we got into a few tussles about my not caring and why would someone evict a person for only being one to two months behind on rent.

One thing I learned is that if people thought being that late on rent was no big deal, I was going to have much bigger problems down the road. This was reminiscent of the guy telling me he would pay the rent when he was ready and really, what was the big deal if he was weeks late? The sad part was this lady was obviously very unhappy. Check out the e-mail.

"I cannot believe that a company would start eviction on someone that is only one month behind. But if that is what you want then whatever. I am trying the best I can. I told you about the $XXXX.00 I lost to a scam. And I am now waiting on the Consumer Affairs for X. XXXXXXX to look into it. I filed a claim with them over a week ago. The reason the check bounced is because something that was not supposed to be deposited was. And your check is not the only thing that bounced. It caused everything to bounce. And my husband XXXXXXXX. But I know you don't care, so why am I telling you anything. I don't get paid until Friday the second. That is the best I can do. I am going through enough headache and heartache to have you and your company threatening me all the time."

No, read that again. She got scammed, and we have to suffer for it. Then she obviously wrote some check to someone and hoped it wouldn't be cashed, so that is our fault also. Amazing cash management skills she has.

Listen, let's be real. She is not a rocket scientist, plain and simple. Who does what she does? They just lost their house and I forgive the debt and they should get a bonus because I am the idiot thinking helping them would be good. Oh no. She has to go find another $5K (*scam*) the day after we pay off her lien and execute the lease. I can't fathom why she would want to borrow another $5K right away and do what with it? She actually send money to someone online who promised to return her $5,000.00 in a loan. I just wanted to scream, but who cares, she just wants the money, someone did her a solid and she wants more cash.

Seriously this is a where I quietly sink back into my chair and just whisper to myself. "*You can deal with stupid stuff like this.*" It takes time to develop this sort of idiocy in your life. We help to get you out of more debt and then you send money to some fly by night group to secure a new $5,000 loan because I just bailed you out of one $10,000.00 loan and then when it doesn't work out you spin blame on your landlord? Get out of dodge!! Who does that to someone immediately after reducing your debt and liabilities? Only in America! The part that gets me is somehow this is our fault and we shouldn't get the rent because she fell for a scam. Plus, I don't like this concept of saying that I threaten people. I am very upfront and tell them what is happening from the beginning. You know how some folks can be so sweet and then hit the crazy switch? This lady had the whole house set up with those switches!

If you don't pay rent or your mortgage, foreclosure and eviction is not a threat, it is a reality. You cannot be continually behind in rent and expect landlords that pay the mortgage, insurance, taxes, maintenance and other expenses on the house and just smile when you decide to not pay the rent. Landlords, I know you're out there hooting and hollering, "YEAH! That happens to me all the time!"

There is more on this great borrower later; she is a 3-year story and ¾ of an inch in emails. Crazy lady and seriously not right in the head.

This is a business for us, this is my salary. Not one of these people would take kindly to their employer saying to hang on for a month to get paid. Yeah right, they would be knocking down the doors of their employer, protesting, you name it. They would be sitting with the loons defecating in the park in NY with the occupy Wall Street crowd. They would be in the streets with placards and yelling obscenities. The message I have for some in this country is that you shouldn't push your inability to make good financial decisions onto someone else. Accept it and make good on your obligations, but so many are conditioned to being behind their whole lives and expecting a bailout over and over again. This borrower/renter I think had a good heart and intentions, until maybe age 5, and then just had too many tough years behind her. Her personal relationship situation doesn't seem to be going well either. She would complain that her spouse was a drunk, but when he would approach our representatives 'drunk and angry' she would then say,

"Who told you he was a drunk?" and then start hitting the crazy switches.

Listen, I was doing everything I could to be patient about having her catch up on rent and it was my hope that she actually repurchased the home. Screeeeech!!! Hit the brakes. Nine months later I am kicking the crazy women out of the house. She hasn't paid in three months and now I am no longer compassionate. Nope, I'm "mean and ugly." That is what you get called if you don't give someone a free pass on rent nowadays after forgiving their mortgage arrears over $17,000.00 and paying off a second lien for them. Ungrateful borrower and renter in this situation. She did inquire about reducing the price of the home, and then complained it wasn't worth the amount owed and then blah blah blah. Everyone wants us to take a loss on money they used to do something other than its original purpose. And check this out, oh yes I'm going to write it, a new car in the driveway! How does that happen? OMG!!! She is that lady: Sitting in the car dealers' office signing the papers, while on her cell phone with me explaining she will miss her monthly rent payment. Get the heck out of dodge!

She eventually sent me a email complaining that her finances were upside down and couldn't make the rent. I even gave her a month pause during Christmas. She called me and said it was Christmas and I reminded her it was yes, Christmas for me also. She didn't hear that part, she just didn't want to pay the rent in December and asked to delay it until Jan 1, which I stupidly did and months later was working with the attorney to get December, January through March. It turns out she bought a new car that with insurance that exceeded $900 a month. NO kidding! Yea, she is in the throes of three years in foreclosure and rent eviction issues and she buys a new ride for well over the monthly home rent. Stupid is as stupid does.

Her excuse was that she was a woman and they took advantage of her. Yep, they shot her with a dart gun to tranquilize her in the street and when she work up she had signed the paperwork for a slick new ride. I heard this happens all the time in the concrete jungle. Come on man!

NEVER A DULL MOMENT

To cap off an exciting day that June, I dealt with a favorite borrower who loved to talk and write, but was always behind and was working diligently to try and come up with money to get current and work to fix their credit issues. You have to root hard for these types of folks to succeed, and I actually enjoyed the constant email updates, which was fantastic, since borrowers not returning calls, letters emails and even not speaking with me was the first hurdle I had to overcome. Most just ignore my calls and emails. Still, reading the struggles they go through just to pay for their home is tough. However, I also know that there are real families behind the money that is behind the home, and they worked hard to earn it and no one should require them to just walk away from their hard work regardless how dire someone's situation is. We just had to choose our families first, plain and simple.

I tended to get interesting emails on a regular basis describing what this borrower in particular wanted to do and how large the upcoming payments would be. It never turned out like their intentions implied, never.

I read all the letters and emails, read the notes that our Loan Servicer posts in the database. I think at times, how can you read this stuff and not root for them to succeed?

Personally, I think they will have success and I just have to have patience at this point. It is hard to fault those that make the effort, but many don't want to make the difficult and responsible attempt to get their finances in order. Even if you have a legitimate emergency, you still have to make some tough choices instead of expecting others, such as us, to finance the emergency (e.g. the car break down, serious medical situation, etc.) Sad but true. We are families and that request to forgive a payment is a request for us personally to give you money straight from our bank accounts. No can do anymore. I know that many times I have been fed a line of bst and people make up stories about tragedy. Borrowers find that pulling on the heartstrings with lies tends to buy them some time and sometimes additional money. Some of them are excellent at it, but even the good ones run out of mothers dying and explanations about surgeries, that, to be honest with you, don't make sense, such as... "A stent from the brain to the stomach?" Is that even possible? And why?

In retrospect I look back and think, if I was losing my home, would I lie, steal and cheat to try and gain every advantage I could to ask the lender to forgo thousands upon thousands of dollars I used for personal gain or pleasure that were legally and rightfully theirs? Right now I say no, but unless put in that situation, I guess one doesn't know what they would actually do. Thinking this, I have so much more respect for those borrowers who dealt with me in an honest fashion and made every attempt to make things right and fought to clean up their financial record in hopes of getting a new, clean mortgage and starting afresh. To those I say, "Thank you." To the others, I say, "Oh my Lord, what were you thinking?"

COLORADO: HOME SWEET HOME?

Colorado is where we live, play and work. We don't have much business in Colorado, but we had to take a home in Colorado in 2009. This is one where I sent letters to the borrower, tried calling, everything in hopes of working a deal, however I failed to make contact prior to the foreclosure sale. This guy had considerable equity in the property, but was not paying anything; no taxes, no insurance, you name it. We were on the hook for everything, so he left us no choice but to foreclose on the home.

Once the sale was made, I knocked on the door and made myself out to be a contractor there to check on clean-up (yes, sometimes even I have to be sneaky to get into a property we own). Wow. The place was disgusting. I don't know how people lived that way. After we spent around $5,000 to fix it up, we sold it for a good margin. This guy left about $40k on the table. They don't listen do they, sell your home yourself if you have equity.

I sure wish I had more of those, but mostly the exact opposite in this market and economy. As for the homeowner who lost the home and that refused to work with me, maybe he did not have any cash or smarts to fix or clean the place. But that is still very ignorant on his part? These people need to make the smart decisions, especially when your lender is telling you to sell the property and not let them take the equity. If you don't want to do that, and you want to fight throughout the whole process, then we will take the equity. That equity gives us the funding to balance against other losses and helps us in fighting other cases where people do nothing but attempt to delay the legal process. Was this guy stupid? Being politically incorrect, I would have to definitely say, Yes!

Initially we rented this home and this gave me my first very real rental experience in this business. I did remember showing the place to a couple and leaning up against the water heater, as I put my hand down I felt something under my palm. I turned to look, while talking to this couple and it seems the previous owner forgot one of his porn pictures of a really overfed lady (that was politically correct, right?) he obviously knew very well. It was actually a Polaroid shot. Wow, I didn't know anyone used those anymore. I had to hide my shock and pocket that bad boy quickly (no, I don't still have it for reminiscence).

Anyhow, one couple I spoke with struck me as nice and needed a place to move their family, so they could move out of their parent's home. Clean people; jobs checked out. They seemed to have good renter potential. I meet them to exchange keys, copy of the lease, and receive the cash, deposit, first and last month's rent, you know how it goes. Well, sure enough they show up with about half the required amount. This should have been my first clue that this was not going to go as smooth as I had hoped. Yes, I admit, I was too nice. Some might say, *naïve*, some in the rental business would say *stupid*. OK, I was stupid, but come on; I had faith in my fellow man as I started this business. I wasn't jaded yet people, lighten up. In my mind, while trying not to show too much anger about only getting half the money, I was thinking, "OK, he says he will bring it next week, the remainder of the money that is, and I am OK with that." So, I let them move in and learn my first lesson.

Lesson 1-If they don't have the money now, they won't have it tomorrow, no matter what they say.

It was a struggle from day one to get the rent. We went back and forth. I allowed them to break it into two payments to help them manage finances and eventually to pay on a weekly basis. They had two babies and I didn't want to kick them out. It became increasingly obvious, however, just like with our borrowers, that they could not afford this home. Instead of fighting them on this, I offered them $300 to move out and find another place. Yes, I bribed them to move out. I was paying people who owed us money, our own money to yes...get the heck out of our homes!

They had already burned the deposit by not paying rent. She bit on the $300 the day after she told me her husband got arrested for bank robbery. Just Great! I rented to a convicted bank robber. Yikes. OK, so days later I ask if the move was on schedule. "Yes," was the answer, "by the weekend?" Weekend comes and I call again and no move. What is up? Since it was obvious she wasn't going to pay or move until the sky fell or a bomb hit nearby, I had to take action. Since hubby was in jail, I just worked with the woman at this point and figure she needed help to get moving. I told her I would rent a truck, rent one month's worth of a storage unit, and find a crew to move her back to her mom's. She was good with that after telling me her dad was a no good (*insert expletives here*) for not giving her money to help her move, *blah blah blah.* Yeah, anyone that doesn't give you money is horrible. Write that down for future use: Mean and ugly jerks it seems. Come on, we aren't that bad. We must be better than most renters' family. We at least show up to help them move their personal belongings when no one else will. How does that work America?

The interesting and fun part of this story was bringing my friend and boss along for the ride. This is sort of like that one hit wonder 'Undercover Boss.' Problem was he was not undercover. I knew he was there. You know, the boss gets his hands dirty with the employees like me. Boy, were we both in for a surprise. My guys open the door, walk inside, come back out and tell me to join them with a smirk on the faces. I knew something was up. The renter was with us and told me prior that the house was clean and our new carpet was still like new. OH NO IT WASN'T! Time for text language: OMG..#%#!!!! I walk into a home that was housing two babies and get hit with the huge stench of cat and dog piss and poop. OMG yet AGAIN!! If I could put a scratch and sniff right here I would, just so you could get a small inkling of how bad it was. The carpet looked like a small minefield of cat and dog bombs. No kidding, poop and urine everywhere, obviously dried up for months. You couldn't step without hitting something that came out of a dog or cat, or maybe human. Ugh, I sure hope not. Kudos to our carpet guy who that week cleaned it up in an amazing fashion, the guy has supernatural powers. He is an absolute MAGICIAN!!

This isn't over yet! We go downstairs and it seems although the house had a huge backyard that was gated, the dogs never spent time outside. No poop on the lawn, but tons of bombs in the basement. Ok, not a pile or two, I am telling you there seemed to be more poop piles than there was open floor. It was every 2-3 inches in the basement. About this time I wanted to call 'Mean Jerk Dad' and shake his hand for saying no to his daughter. Instead, I yelled for the renter to come down and clean it up. We used a snow shovel down there to scoop it up. She thought nothing of it. In fact, she has clothes down there with dog and cat droppings all over them. That got boxed up and went to storage, poop and all. Yeah, what a mess.

Then we hit the garage where it seems the dog and the trash spent their complete life when not dropping bombs in the house. What the heck did they feed these animals? Here is an exceptionally good part of the story. They also decided to not pay for trash pickup, so three months of trash, medicines, dirty diapers and the dog and his golden treasures were in one space. Yes!!! For three months. The dog shredded every bag and both my friend and I waded into about 18 inches of trash and excrement, evenly strewn across the whole garage floor. It was actually impressive how all this stuff seemed to be spread evenly across the garage. Impressive skills that dog must have had. The reek and mess was unbearable to say the least. You wanted to grab the renter by the throat and push her face into the mess. More so because it wasn't just her and her criminal spouse in this filth, she in fact allowed two young children to live in this freaking pigpen. Disgusting people! I have to note that the husband called me to thank for helping her when he was in prison. Not one sorry about the mess they left though.

America, listen up now. These are the folks our Government wants us to help get into a home or save from eviction. You have got to be kidding me. The lessons about people just kept piling on. The good news, we decided no more renters in this home and sold that property as noted earlier.

It is noteworthy that my boss no longer wanted pictures of homes we foreclosed on, nor was he interested in going to see any of them at this point. He got the point loud and clear and didn't need to see the these properties anymore. It did take some of my thunder away. But now, it was only I who was blessed with all the pleasant memories to come. I am so lucky to have been consecrated in this fashion. These memories are not something I go to when I go to my happy place.

This first house was like boot camp and it prepared me for the rest of my dealing with the rest of our deadbeat nation. I was moving forward with a new perspective. Yep, sure enough, people were disgusting!

MY HOME VS FAST FOOD

As a normal course of business I have borrowers who request breaks on their loans. I cannot fault them for trying, I guess. As a matter of routine you can ask and get evidence of finances so we could review the situation in full and decide if we do want to make changes. Our policy is a broad, no modification policy, but I do review them as they come up, in case something is there that changes my mind. Usually, this is not the case.

I have learned that this review of a borrower's finances doesn't matter much anymore. At this point, I focus more on having total finances in the whole portfolio under control and the fact that we normally don't give loan modifications, or attempt to even cut rates to well below what is our borrowing rate, is where I now make my stand.

It has come to the point where it is just not my problem to worry anymore about all these folks not being able to manage their income and time and time again I see that they spend every dime they have, and yet want to borrow more. Why? Because this Country has allowed financial irresponsibility to be an acceptable practice. Entitlement spending is the best example. It just keeps growing when people want more and more of what is not theirs. Even when we review finances, you see not just the total influx of cash and outflow of expenses, but you see distinctly how poorly people manage the income they receive. I am not about to lower rates so folks can afford that new car, or private school, or excessive nights out on the town. It is not prudent to give that many breaks to high risk borrowers for things they can do without, or things they should do without, when they are in a financial bind and are financially blind. But try telling that to people. The sad depressed tone in their voice moves to anger and indignation as they jump through the phone at you. I say, don't call and ask me for more of my money, or to relieve yourself of an obligation, if you cannot honestly discuss how you spend your money. Go knock on someone else's door.

Usually the information provided to us will include bank statements, employment stubs, and other loan documents, anything that showed their financial situation. I had one of those days reviewing a borrower who wanted some break on their loan. They had sent me the last month of their bank statements. I found it interesting. In this case we had a family struggling to pay us $1,200 a month and needing some help (couldn't we just cut the payment some more?). A close look at a bank statement showed some interesting habits and swayed me away from thinking they really only had $10 left at the end of the month. They brought their checking account to our attention, but what they failed to note was how they got into this situation, through some poor spending habits. Check out a blacked out copy of the bank statement I received. Notice anything?

CHASE ○

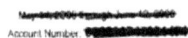

Account Number:

DEPOSITS AND ADDITIONS

DATE	DESCRIPTION		AMOUNT
05/18	US Treasury 220 Tax Refund	PPD ID:	$295.00
05/23	US Treasury 220 Tax Refund	PPD ID:	600.00
05/28	US Treasury 303 Soc Sec	PPD ID:	1,377.00
05/30	Public Safety Pension	PPD ID:	1,966.11
06/03	US Treasury 312 Soc Sec	PPD ID:	1,049.00
Total Deposits and Additions			**$5,287.11**

ATM & DEBIT CARD WITHDRAWALS

DATE	DESCRIPTION		AMOUNT
05/14	Card Purchase 06/12 Texas Rohse Holdings L Phoenix AZ Card 7131	1	$68.12
05/16	Card Purchase W/Cash 05/15 Frys Food & Drug 6802 I Phoenix AZ Card 7149 Purchase $23.54 Cash Back $20.00		43.54
05/16	Card Purchase 06/14 Valley Eye Specialists Phoenix AZ Card 7149		10.00
05/19	Card Purchase With Pin 05/18 Wal-Mart #3465 Glendale(W) AZ Card 7149		60.00
05/19	Card Purchase With Pin 05/18 Net K'mart 5600 Tolleson AZ Card 7149		50.31
05/19	Card Purchase With Pin 06/17 Sou Best Buy #1109 5317 Avondale AZ Card 7131		17.40
05/19	Card Purchase With Pin 05/17 Wal-Mart #1549 Phoenix AZ Card 7131		16.10
05/19	Card Purchase 05/16 Quiznos 3490 Q22 Phoenix AZ Card 7131	2	15.12
05/19	Card Purchase 05/15 Arby's #806 00008060 Tolleson AZ Card 7149	3	14.12
05/20	Card Purchase 05/19 Sainz Mexican Restauran Phoenix AZ Card 7131	4	15.97
05/21	Card Purchase With Pin 05/20 Frys Food & Drug 6602 I Phoenix AZ Card 7149		39.93
05/21	Card Purchase 05/20 Quiznos 3490 Q22 Phoenix AZ Card 7149	5	20.62
05/22	Card Purchase 05/21 Hobby Bench # 5 Glendale AZ Card 7149		27.68
05/22	Card Purchase With Pin 05/21 Frys Food & Drug 6602 I Phoenix AZ Card 7149		20.00
05/22	Card Purchase 05/21 Nf*Www.Netflix Com/ Netflix.Com CA Card 7149		18.37
05/23	Non-Chase ATM Withdraw 05/22 *Harkins-Gateway Pavili Avondale AZ Card 7149	6	42.00
05/23	Card Purchase 05/22 Fuddruckers #256 Glendale AZ Card 7149	7	24.67
05/23	Card Purchase 05/22 Retinal Consultants of Phoenix AZ Card 7131		10.00
05/27	Card Purchase With Pin 05/23 Wal-Mart #3465 Glendale(W) AZ Card 7149		150.45
05/27	Card Purchase With Pin 05/26 Wal-Mart #1549 Phoenix AZ Card 7149		76.50
05/27	Card Purchase 05/22 Applebee S 5100005185 Goodyear AZ Card 7149	8	38.47
05/27	Card Purchase 05/22 Park Central Deli- Phoenix AZ Card 7149	9	23.22
05/28	Card Purchase 05/26 The Olive Gard00017188 Phoenix AZ Card 7131	10	47.90
05/28	Card Purchase 05/27 Quiznos 3490 Q22 Phoenix AZ Card 7149	11	12.76
05/29	Card Purchase 05/28 Psc*Farmers Ins Exc Farmers.Com CA Card 7149		659.56
05/29	Card Purchase 05/28 Public Storage 08011 75 AZ Card 7149		155.43
05/29	Card Purchase W/Cash 05/28 Frys Food & Drug 6602 I Phoenix AZ Card 7149 Purchase $45.04 Cash Back $20.00		65.04
05/30	Card Purchase 05/29 Alltel *Phone Paymen AR Card 7131		302.44
05/30	Card Purchase With Pin 05/29 Wal-Mart #3465 Glendale(W) AZ Card 7149		190.54
05/30	Card Purchase 05/29 Jb's Restaurant 10 Phoenix AZ Card 7131	12	21.11
06/02	Card Purchase With Pin 06/01 Frys Food & Drug 6602 I Phoenix AZ Card 7149		176.24
06/02	Card Purchase 05/29 Frys #7126 Phoenix AZ Card 7149		62.02
06/02	Card Purchase With Pin 06/01 Frys Food & Drug 6602 I Phoenix AZ Card 7149		58.30
06/02	Card Purchase 05/31 Lim's Chinese Rest #2 Phoenix AZ Card 7131	13	45.08
06/02	Card Purchase 05/31 Carls Jr 7560 Q50 Phoenix AZ Card 7149	14	16.98

Page 3 of 4

70

CHASE O

ATM & DEBIT CARD WITHDRAWALS (continued)

DATE	DESCRIPTION		AMOUNT
06/02			12.66
06/02	Card Purchase With Pin 05/30 Wal-Mart #3465 Glendale(W) AZ Card 7149		47.94
06/04	Card Purchase 06/02 Chroma World Inc 800-8729595 DE Card 7131	15	14.91
06/04	Card Purchase 06/03 Quiznos 3490 Q22 Phoenix AZ Card 7149		212.20
06/05	Card Purchase 06/04 Fic*Foremost Insuran 800-527-390 MI Card 7149		106.97
06/05	Card Purchase With Pin 06/04 Wal-Mart #3465 Glendale(W) AZ Card 7131	16	56.02
06/05	Card Purchase 06/04 Arriba Mexican Grill # Glendale AZ Card 7131		39.93
06/06	Card Purchase 06/05 Goodwill of Central An Phoenix AZ Card 7149	17	23.83
06/06	Card Purchase 06/04 Kitchen Gourmet Glendale AZ Card 7149		109.72
06/09	Card Purchase With Pin 06/07 Wal-Mart #3465 Glendale(W) AZ Card 7149	18	94.58
06/09	Card Purchase 06/05 Red Lobster Us00062182 Phoenix AZ Card 7131	19	38.55
06/09	Card Purchase 06/07 Papa Johns #2967 502-261-4342 AZ Card 7149	20	25.40
06/09	Card Purchase 06/08 Carls Jr 7560 Q50 Phoenix AZ Card 7149	21	22.27
06/10	Card Purchase 06/08 Denny's #6556 Phoenix AZ Card 7131		63.33
06/11	Card Purchase W/Cash 06/10 Frys Food & Drug 6602 l Phoenix AZ Card 7149 Purchase $43.33 Cash Back $20.00		24.00
06/11	Card Purchase With Pin 06/10 Frys Food & Drug 6602 l Phoenix AZ Card 7149	22	23.70
06/11	Card Purchase 06/09 Fuddruckers #256 Glendale AZ Card 7131		$3,529.95

Total ATM & Debit Card Withdrawals

OTHER WITHDRAWALS, FEES & CHARGES

DATE	DESCRIPTION	AMOUNT
05/30	Withdrawal	$1,740.00
		$1,740.00

Total Other Withdrawals, Fees & Charges

[Handwritten notes:] 22 fast food in under 30 days $549 ?? in under 30 days and doesn't include cash.

Ok, so we have over $540 in less than one month for eating out and fast food and then they complain they can't afford the mortgage on the home? They not only wanted us to finance their home, they wanted us to finance their unhealthy eating habits. My guess is the next step for them is to apply for disability at retirement, your social security will pay for these folks when they are unable to work because of weight issues. Is that flippant? Sure, but I am not here to be politically correct. You cannot tell me all the thousands of grossly overweight people claiming disability are that way due to a disease. They just eat too much. Ever see those folks on the carts in the food stores. Take a quick peek at the Spielberg ET basket on the front of the cart and I bet you you will see nutritious stuff like Snack Cakes, soda pop and other fine and healthy quisine.

It is one thing to have a disability from military service, accident or true disease, but it is sad that we Americans end up paying for stuff that people do to themselves, eat like pigs and then needing a motorized cart to move their butts around. Put the snack cakes down people! NOW! Just not right for others to pay for someone to sit around and eat themselves into disability.

No, it is not our position nor responsibilty as a business to monitor food or health, but the same can be said it is not our place to support this lifestyle with reductions to our pocket. Does this sound mean, nah, just that people don't look inside themselves before they claim they need real help. They need to cut back, be responsible and clean house first. They just need to take personal responsibility.

Please oh please, take some responsibily for the mess you are in. Oh, I can have sympathy, but don't lay your financial burdens at my doorstep. Please take care of your personal obligations wihout asking us to sacrifice ours. No, we are not your family. We are in a business relationship folks, plain and simple. It is not fair for us to bear your burden. Is this what you are teaching your children. We hear about the dumbing down of American children all the time and this sort of attitude at home also reaches into what we teach children about personal responsibility. When in doubt, demand someone else bear your burden?

Or maybe folks should exercise some financial self control. That's a concept worth consideration. But again, maybe too many of our borrowers just didn't have the ability to come to the conclusion that they should be responsible for themselves in a society that wants to keep giving them money, that is, taking from those who are responsible and giving to those who are not. It is a vicious circle that may never change. These people are voters and the people that run our country see them as voters that need to be appeased.

Recently I received some more "workout requests" on loans. People in foreclosure. On one I see a $900 mortgage and then see that they have claimed over $450 in cable TV, cell phone and internet billings per month. Ok, who knows my answer here? Come on people! You need a home before you need premium cable and the internet. It isn't a right nor does it seem right to sacrifice your home for those luxuries. Totally unreal.

GIVE THEM A BREAK?

I recently watched a program where a bank was giving deliquent and defaulted borrowers, at risk of foreclosure, a new 2 percent (2%) loan. Again this is a wow! Ok, nice gesture, but what does that say to the people always making their payments at 5-6-7-8 percent, and at even higher percentages, who are not in that risk-level position? They, and we, are thinking, so this is what happens if I don't pay my mortgage? 2 percent! Those who don't pay get a 40-75% cut in their mortgage rate? What a great country, and folks are out there screaming to help the ones not meeting their obligations.

Our Government seems to live off of blaming banks, business and overall corporate America as a distraction to catch the attention of the naïve. It can make you sick if you realize it. It gets back to people not understanding that corporate America is comprised of people, not machines! Look inside first people. Shape up. It's a shame we don't expect more folks to buck up and quit asking for help when you can do so much on your own in just cutting back on expenses. But that is all our Government seems to want to do, increase the welfare portion of our society. Not just those that need it but those that abuse it to no end. Don't blame me for your inability to manage your finances or control your spending.

Recently received a request to forgive all backpayments on a loan and give these folks a new 2 percent loan. Holy cow batman, 2%! Part of their finances show a car payment at $600 per month, and internet at $150 per month. Wow, you are paying $750 a month for a car and internet, but not paying your mortgage? Priorities, get it? Driving some sweet ride no doubt and no way will they give up that status symbol. Ridiculous! Sorry to bring the car scenario back into the picture. It just hovers over this business like a rain cloud!

Sure lets give them a break. This all hits home more and more everyday. I spoke with some close friends of mine who teach and are getting depressed and stressed about their professional choice. I hear them tell me that they are pouring more and more resources into "at risk" classes, such as those attended by kids who really have no interest in going to class. Not a secret. They sit there and ignore everyone and wait for the bell to ring. A waste of time and money. What you don't hear and what they tell me, is that the majority of these "at risk" students are children who don't want to be there in the first place and don't want to learn, but teachers are mandated to spend extra time with them. What about those willing to learn? Why not provide them the attention they have earned? We are learning early that if you don't show responsibility for yourself you tend to get the majority of the attention and money regardless. No wonder our education system is failing with massive increases of capital over the decades that has not resulted in a better education system. Our educational system is broken. Additional funding will not solve the problem. Giving schools more money doesn't make them better, any more than giving money to folks who poorly manage their personal finances makes them better. Pretty simple, but the government doesn't get it. Oh, yea, these are voters. My bad.

"Takers" just continue to take. They take, move on and keep coming back to the trough to ask for more and then whine about their situation.

This will never end and those that work diligently and bust their ass will be asked day in and day out to forego much of their hard-earned dollars. The workers are the ones expected to give to the folks sleeping late, eating all day or the gang-banger that got shot in a scuffle and claims he cannot work anymore and is now on Social Security. Yep it happens. System is what it is...screwed up people.

STROLL THROUGH FLORIDA

Early on, during my adventure as a virgin small family lender, my wife and I took a two week trip to Florida. The plan was to meet the borrowers, give them a small gift, check out the houses and allow myself to get familiar with these folks I was talking to almost daily. The intention was to let them know that we weren't a big bad bank, but we were but a small group of folks who had given them money to play with and are now trying to keep the investment alive.

This trip also showed that we were very capable of being able to reach out and touch you, like the old telephone commercial. What an experience that was! We saw houses that were in total disrepair, but somehow they managed to afford vehicles such as Hummers, Mercedes and BMW's and parked them proudly outside of trashed houses that they considered their home. This has nothing to do with the size and location of the home; I'm talking the home exterior, the yard, and the majority of the time, the interior of the home. What a mess we saw at times.

We had the pleasure of visiting one of our borrower's homes that was worth around $140K. It was gated with a GM Hummer, (or do the Chinese own that now as well?) BMW and a van parked in the yard.

By the way, why do so many people park in the grass in Florida? Is there a state law there about sidewalks and driveways? Driveways are not a big deal for some reason.

So riddle me this Batman. How can you afford those newer cars and be behind in your mortgage on a $100K plus home? Is it just a matter of priorities and keeping the home is not one of them? Head shake... maybe a nod of confusion, shake of disbelief...and then the realization of, yep, this is the case, crazy right!

I know you have heard this before, but again, this is my book. Experience has taught me that many people cherish other material possessions more than their home...surprising and ridiculous, but fact. I can see them at the dinner table?

"Honey is the mortgage due?

Well, darling, I really had my eyes on a new set of 22 inch gold plated rims for the Hummer and dual DVD players in the back seat for our Friday night out with the neighbors, what do you say about us skipping the mortgage and getting those today with some new tread and then taking a plane to Hawaii for some fun?

Oh, honey, that is why I love you so much, you are so smart and always thinking ahead. Let's do it. We can always get Government assistance to keep the house and cry that the big bad bank is kicking us out. It worked for Betty and Ted next door."

FYI (the disclaimer): This is a fictional conversation, I really didn't overhear it.

OK, so I make light of it, but what the heck were they talking about before they stepped into the dealership and laid their John Hancock signature on the line for that expensive loan or lease on the premium vehicle? Zoom Zoom, Yippee, look at me!

When I first wrote this back in 2010, I was somewhat dismayed and shocked. Hell, nothing stuns me anymore. I wouldn't be surprised to see 10 luxury autos parked in front of a home worth $100,000 that we would be foreclosing on. Nope, wouldn't make me blink at all. I would laugh and say, "I told you so!"

Remember the previous story of the borrower who became a renter and then bought a car exceeded her monthly rent. She certainly had the gall to say this; *'I was a woman and they took advantage of me'*. Give me a break. If I had hair, I would pull it out when I heard that. If you expect people to believe that, then you are at the top of the idiot pile in this country.

Did they run out in the street and pull her in and then hold a gun to her head to sign for a NEW CAR when she was in the throes of potentially losing her home. Everyone reading this knows quite well what happened. She reduced her living expenses at our expense and immediately went out to spend that extra money. At this point I say good riddance to people like that. I just tire of taxpayers and us being coerced and cheated into helping these people pay their bills.

There is a point in your life where you either have the thing you want or you live with the reasons why you don't.

PLAY BALL

I have one Florida home visit etched in my mind more than others. The sun was scorching out and we were using the GPS to find one of the first properties after getting to Miami. We pulled down the street and come upon the address. The house actually looked decent, thought the neighborhood didn't look very 'kid' friendly, and the home is gated like a mini Fort Knox. And right in the spirit with my experiences on a $100K homes, there is a Mercedes SUV in the drive. The mortgage payment is under $1,200 per month and these folks aren't paying. No doubt the Mercedes and associated insurance is expensive, and so might be the maintenance on the nice iron fence around the property. No time for paying the mortgage, we have other things to purchase.

So, I rang the bell on the gate and was not surprised no one answered. Then, I start to look around.

Here is a picture I can paint for you of me visiting this home. I'm a big guy with a shaved head, wearing shorts and casual shirt buzzing the gate. My beautiful wife in her cute shorts is walking around taking photos of the property. Then I look to the left and see a group of men, not boys, milling around about 50 yards down the street from where we were parked and walking around.

Of course this is in the middle of the day. How do you get this many men together in one spot during the middle of the day or do they all work the night shift?

They notice us, but do nothing but watch us. What got me was two of them had baseball bats in their hands. Ok, I know it is warm in Florida in August, and it's baseball season, but I am seeing no ball, no gloves and these guys are in jeans, or jean shorts and sandals, they are not wearing cleats or playing a friendly game of catch, and no one is yelling, "hum-baby- hum, throw it in there." They were not really looking like any baseball team I have ever seen.

So, using my better judgment, I motioned to my wife to finish up and let's move on. Even in the loan business, you have to know when to fold 'em, and when to move on and use third party support for door knocks!

REAL ESTATE AND LEGAL BUMS

Even our wealthier or seemingly wealthier borrowers had some screws loose. I was dealing with one loose screw for a few years. He is another one of those who decided he didn't have to pay and obviously expected us to support him. This one became a court matter.

During Mediation the borrower wanted what worked out to less than a zero percent (0%) interest loan from us. I did learn that opposing counsel can never do the math nor do they want too. Were they shocked and dismayed that we wouldn't do a principle reduction and not offer him a less that 0% note? Crazy attorney? Yes, crazy like a fox. Some attorneys will press any absurd motion or deal since they get paid regardless. However, don't pay them and they'll walk away and abandon these oh so poor borrowers who need help. So corny to hear the legal representatives' supposed compassion for so many who had no intention of paying their loan and being so full of bull.

With this borrower, he was able to hire counsel and fought us tooth and nail all the way to the courtroom. Eventually, he lost his counsel and tried fighting on his own. He was a real estate developer and owed his partners money, and wanted us to also take it in the shorts rather than take responsibility for the bad investments he made. It is a beautiful house in Plantation, Florida with million dollar homes on the street. The first few times I spoke with him I tried to make a deal. He would agree, and then I wouldn't hear from him or get any money. Took me longer than it should have to realize I was being played, but I wanted to give him and his wife a chance. You just want people to honor commitments and work things out, but it doesn't happen that way in real life. For the first few years of our battle, he wanted us to agree to a reverse mortgage and settle for about a $250K second on the house for us. We were and are under water with this guy to the tune of over $800,000.00. No way we were going to put ourselves in a second mortgage position on the property and have a junior lien on a house. This situation wasn't good business, and it wasn't going to happen anytime and anywhere. We ended up in a shouting match at each other because I wouldn't give him what he wanted. I just can't understand why people expect us to take huge financial hits on their behalf. This just doesn't compute.

This guy had pretty much disappeared behind his lawyers. Cutting business deals with people who don't honor their obligations, or fight to try and make you give up tons of money, does not endear them to me, nor incline me to continue to make business propositions with them. There comes a time when you just want the house back and the occupants gone.

On this drive around Florida, I found him home and called him from his long driveway (thankfully he did have a driveway). I asked him about the color of his home and some other small talk. I was actually surprised he answered my call, so the small talk was necessary to relieve him of the initial surprise. I got a long measurable silence when I told him the house looked good. Hmmm, I don't think he figured I would ever reach out and touch him, but I did! He then knew who I was and was pleasant and invited me in. We talked about the old deals on the table.

Nothing came of the visit, since he ended up complaining to his attorney about me being in Florida and calling him. I was stopped backing out of the driveway by a nice plantation police officer. She informed me about current status with this property, activities going on and wanted to know what I was doing there. We had a long talk that told me our borrower was under other watchful eyes. About 6 months after this, he told the courts he had no idea who I was or even that we owned the loans. Flat out lied. Amazing what people will say and do and not think twice about it. All I had to do was provide phone records of our calls and copies of letters he sent direct to me to show he was lying to the courts. People lie so easily, and in our case people would lie to try and put us on the defensive as the big bad bank. Truth is lying from our borrowers doesn't affect the courts. They ignore it. I did pretty well defusing that situation by explaining we were a small family group and had our own problems, disabilities, job losses, etc. That seemed to help in understanding we were people too and that we just couldn't give money away.

People need to understand that behind the small lender, the small bank, the big bank, or anyone lending money is that there are normal everyday people, neighbors who are shareholders in those banks and who have money invested and expect to earn a return. Media tends to demonize anyone making money in this country but heaven forbid they look at themselves in this way. On this home I eventually had to fire our counsel due to the fact they blew the first foreclosure sale. In their lack of diligence to make sure the sale was ready to go through, they never confirmed with the county clerk on one piece of paper, a piece of paper that stopped the sale from being posted and to this day has caused me to lose over two years since that failed sale date. Since I personally would email the legal team numerous times about everything being in place, there were no excuses. I would always ask if the sale was ready to go. They only picked up the phone to verify the error with the courts, AFTER the sale date was blown, and when I called to ask if we got the house back. This error cost us an additional year of taxes, insurance and the borrower got free housing due to the great legal system we have here in America.

Eventually we did get ANOTHER sale date, but this clown borrower filed bankruptcy the day of the sale. Many months, years, later we are still working on removing the property from the bankruptcy filing and getting ownership and a foreclosure sale date. Going over 4 years now. So what will happen? Who knows, but I want that one back to start generating revenue. This barrower has a steady monthly income so they can find a decent place to live, and they'll be just fine without living off us. They can get off my back, since I already have back problems and they are becoming heavy dead weight to carry.

For these types of folks, we have to press them on being responsible for their loan or take the home back. No two ways about it. Eventually this will go to foreclosure sale and then the eviction story will be written, which I gather will also be very interesting and probably combative. Who knows at this point? They may surprise us and leave in the middle of the night and I would be willing to rent the moving truck for them.

Florida was a tough place during my visit of the homes in the loan portfolio. Values were down and some of the neighborhoods were not the best. I got lots of "looks" there. I had folks driving by asking me what I was doing there. These were young men making those types of comments that could be construed as threatening. You were dealing with different cultures, Cuban, Black, Palestinian, White, Hispanic, Venezuelan, you never knew what the course of the discussion would take, or if I could even understand what the looks meant. Was it because I had a different look, or people thought I was a cop, or maybe knew I was the lender? Who knows? The fact was that I was there to do my job and I waved and said hello to anyone around. At that point I also realized that no one trusts anyone in their neighborhood that doesn't look like them, even as a white male in a white neighborhood. Did I belong there?

WEEKLY PRISON CALL

Another Florida borrower just dried up like water in the Sahara when it came to payments. I had difficulty in making contact. No response to calls or emails for months. Turns out the guy was facing prison for shooting someone in the head. Great! We found out it was self-defense, but he was under some sort of parole that required he not own a gun. Catch 22? Not allowed to have a gun, but without the gun he could have been killed. Probably a good tradeoff in his mind.

Well, I tried to contact his wife with no results. Eventually his brother called and said parole's wife was leaving the country and returning home. In that case I offered to pay cash for the deed to help them move. Nothing ever came of it until months later I got a call from a lawyer who routinely helped folks in that community and said someone else was willing to step up and sign on for the house, refinance, etc. I put him in touch with a broker and again nothing happened. Eventually, the initial borrower used his one call per week to contact me from prison and over a few calls we cut a deal for his family to stay on the property, at least a few months until after he got out of prison and would have an opportunity to buy the house back. Not sure any other lender would be making jailhouse calls to keep a family in a home, but we are different and it makes for great story (oh yeah, remember we are bad people). I am hoping he succeeds, since he promised me a drink when we finally meet.

The irony here is he offered me $100K from the prison to pay off the loan. I asked him how he could offer me that kind of money to short sale a home when he couldn't come up with the Mortgage payment. He simply said, *good point* and laughed. Would have been no deal anyway, he owed us close to $200k and we would hold it until the market got better or he suddenly got some morals and paid us what he owed. I believe he used the refinance money to finance his business. This was his choice, and now ours to hold the property. We will see how the story ends next year when he gets released from prison. In the interim, his wife has been making timely rental payments through a property management firm. Things are peachy!

In Florida, our borrowers were chefs, school teachers, government workers, real estate investors, agents, energy workers, doctors, and felons, you name it we had it. We had people from all walks of society in our portfolio. Most of these folks still had their jobs, so losing employment wasn't the problem. The simple fact is that they could not afford the home the day they signed the papers for a mortgage. Instead they paid off credit cards, took cash for cars, vacations and assorted other debts and enjoyment. Maybe the ratios came out ok, but you cannot look over their shoulders and help determine how to spend other's income, what not to buy and how to save. People just spend whatever they have at the moment and hope things get better. There is a section of society full of folks who have no financial discipline and many of those live in Florida.

It became obvious to me that many people take out a refinance, pay off credit cards, cars and other obligations and then sit there and think,"Wow! I don't have a credit card payment or car payment," and then the cycle starts yet again, without a thought to the higher mortgage payment due to the payoffs. Simple, yet stupid.

MOTHERLY LOVE

I have to talk about one lady in Florida who I considered to be amazing. It was not her who held the loan, but her son and it just so happened that it was the same home he grew up in. However, it was mom that continually communicated with us about how to stay in the home. We tried to help with a refinance but appraisals were lousy in 2009- 2011, particularly in Florida. Not accurate valuations, but that is another book for someone else to write and wait forever for it to be edited.

Eventually we agreed on a deed-in-lieu and somewhat complicated repurchase agreement over five years. We wanted to give her enough time to work with her son and regain value in the home. According to mom, he got into the mess to refinance since someone obviously talked him into this high interest loan, then took advantage of him to pull money out in order to get a new car. Stupid new car disease again. He wanted a new car and this seemed like the best way to do it. Seriously people, this is a silly reason to put a homestead at risk, but you know how I feel about that at this point.

Well Mom was a God send for her son, and us, and in October of 2010 we cut the deal to last 5 years with an option for her to have her or her son buy the home back at what was owed after the lease expired. This one is one in which I surely hope they succced. This woman put so much time, energy and her own money into helping her son save his childhood home. I hope he realizes what he has and takes care of his mother one day.

We are still hoping this works and she and her son are still on our books. I hope to give them a few more years to clean up credit and get a chance to find financing to buy the home back from us. As an update, she was not able to sustain paying for her son, but we executed another lease for him as purely a renter. I have gathered over time and through his contacts with out manager is that he is just an angry man and one who sadly didn't appreciate what his mother was doing for him throughout the years. For him, I have no compassion, but for her I feel truly sad, since she tried and tried hard.

DAMN BILLBOARD LAWYERS

I never thought I would have to stand up and testify in court for a foreclosure. But one home had me flying back to Florida to fight a case in court. This is a property where a borrower seemingly wanted the deal I proposed, but his attorney thought otherwise. True butthead, this lawyer was. I have been to hearings, depositions and finally a trial on a $114K property. What a crock. The whole day of trial is cause for a book all in itself. We actually spent almost an hour discussing a $94 late charge. Seriously counselor? You can't calculate a late charge? But we have four attorneys and a judge in here listening to this trivial mess. Really, next book ok? While the trial judge found in our favor, there is some motion now to rescind all that happened. Of course the lawyers aren't happy with the judge's finding that the borrower owes us money and the judge set a date for foreclosure. So we just keep fighting and he gets 4 years of free rent. Just gotta love attorneys, the justice system, just love them TO DEATH!!!

Florida is ripe with opportunity for us. The majority of our loans are there and the majority of those are in trouble. I have knocked on doors of guys with attempted murder charges, guys in and out of rehab, people in prison who abandoned the properties, it never seems to end. I always try to work a deal, but many times people will eventually speak with me, accept my offers and then disappear or hire some attorney making a mint through foreclosures and promising them a free home and months upon months of free rent. Some lawyers are a pox on this country. Just count how many are in the seat of power in DC. Need I say more? I have so much more time and trouble awaiting me in Florida, years and years and more than a few handfuls of homes that we no doubt will own one day after wading through the legal quagmire.

I have one thing to say about cleaning up the housing mess. Let the foreclosure process run its course and get these things through the system. Let the homes get cleaned up and sold in the marketplace. Nothing good is happening by delaying this process, ABSOLUTELY NOTHING....of course, except attorneys getting paid! Enough said.

WASHINGTON STATE: JUST THE BEGINNING

Our adventures in Washington and more specifically a singular home in Washington, have caused more exasperation and disgust than any other in this business. The whole business around this house was nothing short of bizarre. How does a person manage to stay in a home for almost three years without making a single payment? Well, young lads, the answer again revolves around our wonderful legal system. You see Young Skywalker, in this great country, you start by 'borrowing' tons of money under the auspices of remodeling your house, then lie through your teeth, refuse to make those mortgage payments and then go through every legal excuse you can dig up to avoid the inevitable. While doing this evasive maneuver you burn through all the money and leave in the middle of the night abandoning a property half-finished to families like ours who have to pick up the pieces and pour even more money into cleaning up the mess. Geez, you wonder why it is tough to get a loan. Ok, to make matters worse you end up having a property open to squatters, and that is not a good thing in the wonderful state of Washington.

The house in question was an Everett, Washington property where the loan was originated in May of 2007. The borrower made his payments for five long arduous months. He then ceased making payments and was not ordered out of the house until the foreclosure sale in October of 2009. It took **TWO years** to get a foreclosure sale date on this property and then **another six months** to just get control of the property in April of 2010. This control only happened after we were able to evict his "friends" and squatters on the property.

The delay was due to our trying to actively work out a deal with the borrower to help him out. It took way too long for me to learn to quit bending over backwards to try and help people out. I got my butt whooped so many times trying to help folks; you would think I was a race horse or some guy into kinky stuff. But, we keep trying and keep thinking people are honest. Nah, I really don't think people are honest anymore, I was just hoping they would honor their word now and then.

Sad fact is there are not too many honest folks out there that honor their word, and we work with them time and time again. Most good people are old-school folks who were raised to meet their obligations, not raised to run away or find a technicality to avoid payment. It is pathetic that you cannot trust many people in this country anymore. Thank God for the ones you can!!

I now understand why banks and lenders have to just process the foreclosures to try and regain control of assets. If you don't do this, you waste enormous amounts of time, manpower and money on these loans trying to assist folks who have no intention of ever paying a dime, but are just wading through the process for free rent. After years and maybe decades of assistance, they have come to understand that the system works too slow and they know you won't come looking for them over their debt, too burdensome a process to get real justice.

We extend a helping hand and not only do they bite on it, they cut it off and start chewing on it and then ask for more.

This situation in Washington is where I started to learn that many borrowers were only interested in delaying the actually foreclosure sale and had no interest in keeping the house or making any more payments. The objective of following through on their commitment(s) or keeping their word was non-existent. I spent over six months trying to work a deal with this man. Phone calls and e-mails received no response. Our loan servicer was on him constantly about following through with not much luck whatsoever. We cut a few deals, or so we thought, but he never came through on his end of the bargain. All talk and no action.

It became obvious that he was buying time and only time. He had no intention, like so many others, of making good on his obligation. Finally after months of trying to work with him I pulled the trigger for the foreclosure in June of 2009. Here is an excerpt from the loan notes where our servicer documents communications with the borrower and the deal that I approved was consummated but he never followed through on this.

Servicer Notes in file:

[Servicer] *Aug-05-2009 03:53 PM: [CC] **Everett borrower** stated his attorney recommended he try to work it out with lender; I asked what he could pay a month? Said he can afford $2K; I told him that may not be approved; Asked what is max he can pay? Said $2,500.00 monthly but probably can't afford more than that; explained his foreclosure is proceeding and pending sale date of 10/23/09; I asked if he had good faith payment, said he has $1,500.00 available to him in addition to the payment; advised there is a $425.00 fee that must be paid; also explained that lender will not forgive difference in reduction, it is just placed in unpaid interest bucket which will be due at end of loan; however he has the option to refinance at later date, should lender agree to these terms. He understood and said it would be great to get this offer approved by lender. I informed him that lender may not approve however I will stay in touch with him to advise either way. He said he couldn't wait to hear from me.*

Now, reading this he seemed excited about taking this deal, right? He was informed the deal was acceptable and we pushed the proper papers to his attention. I should have known better. Here was a borrower, with a job, but who didn't pay for years, and who took out a considerable amount of cash on the home and had nothing to show for it. No cash reserves? Not sure what these folks do with the mortgage payment they are not making? Eat out at the steakhouse every night? Needless to say it got very quiet on his end and he never followed through on his part of the deal.

Eventually he filed Bankruptcy (BK) and like a child, he stated to an agent representing us with a deed-in-lieu offer, the following comment (and sung to the tune of nanny ♪ nanny ♪ boo ♪ boo ♪) "I filed BK, I filed BK!" What a clown. That is when you know it becomes your mission to do whatever it takes and take the house away from him. The problem is the legal system sounds and works like Slingblade (guy in the movies). It is process heavy, which means slow and methodical. The system doesn't give a damn about the small people who actually loaned the money out. It is all about the folks not following through on the deal they struck. Now, if this was someone legitimately working to actually be honest and straight forward in saving their home, we would continue to work with them, but this guy was a jerk, pure and simple and he needed to be living in a van, down by the river, or his truck in a deep ditch.

The amount of email traffic this guy amassed was amazing. But the whole situation was like watching a runaway train and you have no control over stopping it, each time it comes around the bend, you just throw a wad of money at it and hope it gets stuck on the track, but you know in your mind that there is no way that paper can stop that train…choo choo!!

To cut to the chase, we eventually get the foreclosure sale date and then we get the house back in sale and now have to work on getting the bum off the property. This is much easier said than actually done. Now we have to get to another attorney, put down a retainer and try and evict him through the courts. Nothing is simple, and for sure, that is double the case in Washington State, which seems to love their squatters, unless of course they are in your backyard, but more on that later.

To give you an idea of what the borrower had done to OUR house when he took out this large cash out refinance, read the email from an independent agent that checked out the property.

-----Original Message-----

*From: T**** B*****
<****@*******associates.net>
To: [redacted]
Sent: Fri, 13 Mar 2009 12:14 am
Subject: Everett WA
Good Evening *******,*

How is your evening treating you? Well I hope and thank you again for the opportunity. I had a chance to take some pictures of the property (attached) and take an over view of the condition of the property.

*Download:
http://www.*****************.net/wp-content/uploads/2009/03/pictures.zip*

Exterior

Looking at the property it has some major exterior construction defects. **(Ok defects? It is missing walls buddy!!!)**

It looks as if construction was started and never completed. For example; in picture #1 it can be observed there is no front entry way and is currently covered by think black plastic (I didn't look into the interior) and the siding has been removed on part of the daylight basement. In addition, the front porch stairs have been removed and the concrete base is fully exposed and the wrap around porch of the house has been removed, can be viewed in the historical picture #7 (found it on the NWMLS). **(So..lets see… the $300K was never put into the home, surprise!!)**

Pool

I could not get any pictures of the pool so its condition is unclear but the exterior condition of the pool house looks in decent shape.

Boundary Dispute

The next door neighbor came out and chatted for a bit and shared some information. According to the neighbor the back property had been subdivided and sold off and current he is having an attorney review the documents because he thinks he was screwed. I am still waiting on a title report to determine if these items are accurate.

Residents

According to the neighbor, again, no one has lived in the home for some time and after survey the grounds it looks as if there may be a squatter on the premises. On the eastside of the home there is homemade power line hidden by debris that stretches from the power pole to a back corner window and enters the home.

CMA

Due to the condition of the home and the boundary line information, I want to discuss the CMA with my broker to make sure my findings are correct and provide the CMA tomorrow.

That is all at the moment and the CMA will be in your inbox in the morning. Again, thank you for the opportunity and will talk shortly.

Warmest Regards,

****

Good lord, the place was a wreck. An absolute wreck. We knew over $100K in rehab was going to have to go into this home if we planned on getting anything out of it. People can be such buttholes. Take all this money and just snort it away or blow it on luxuries. Please america, help him out. Right!

WASHINGTON STATE: PART DUEX, SQUATTERS RULE!

So we have a trashed property to look forward to now. Then the fun starts. We try to evict this guy and turns out he scampered away. But...not before he supposedly makes a lease with some vagrants and they claim he took cash from them for rent. So I have this batch of people on the property, who have no legal rights in my opinion, and they claim they have a lease with the old borrower, which they cannot produce and then the trouble starts.

I was wondering what to do at this point, besides sending more money to attorneys. So, just for fun, I contacted a good friend in the state to see if he had someone looking to make some cash who could knock on the door. Turns out his daughter was dating a large, ex-football player, who just so happened to be in law school. Hey, great combination, big physical guy with some schoolin', but too bad it is in Law School! But let's give it a try. (Turns out to be a great young man, BTW) So I sent my young apprentice out to the house. Here is his email summary of the place.

Hey XXXX,

*Good adventure! So as I pulled up I saw four cars in the driveway along with two tweekers in the driveway who were "methed out" of their minds. Naturally, they inquired as to why I was there and I informed them that I was there on your behalf to document the property. I asked where ****** was, and a man named XXX ****** informed me (he was most likely lying* *through his butt), that* ***** *had left for xxxxx xxxxxx, California because his mother had terminal cancer.* **(Damn need to add this post haste to my excuse list).** *At this point I neither believed this nor cared.*

Here are some more wonderful documented photos of the property.

The email from the young man continued:

He also told me that he had a valid lease and that Xxxx the tenant had signed a lease to him for the property. However, I don't think that he realizes that someone who doesn't own a home doesn't have a legal right to sign a lease to third parties. The house is fairly beat up as you will see. The issues that I found are as follows:

- Garbage around the house everywhere and buckets and burn piles

- Looks as if they attempted to do a half butt remodel and left everything in the yard

- Siding is beat up and needs to be painted

- Looks as if a stove has been removed and place along side the house

- The siding is missing around the front door as the pics will point out

- The back porch is collapsing and the railing is almost gone as the pics will point out

- The house currently has no power or water as I was informed, they didn't know why (weird)

- As I saw there are four people living there (3 males, 1 female) and a child (CPS?)

- They also had three dogs at the property

I took pictures of the vehicles and two of the license plates when no one was looking, I don't know if they will be of any help but it can't hurt.

We later found out that they were doing drugs in the house as evidenced by the mess, needles and a hidden room for growing weed and a wonderful smell in the place.

At about this time in the process I received a call from a neighbor to the property. The neighbor had located me through the county records and was worried about the behavior and actions of the tenants in the place, and she was very fearful. Her call was basically to find out what I was going to do about it. I then had contact with another neighbor on the other side of the property and they had the same concerns about the folks in our house. We had many talks with these neighbors about the state of Washington giving more rights to squatters than the folks that own property. They were in disbelief that I couldn't just march in there and physically remove these vagrants. I couldn't believe it either. I think it is time to get back to old school ways and let us do our "Walking Tall" imitation and strut into those houses with a big piece of lumber and order them the hell out of our house!

My discussions with the neighbors would revolve around bitching about idiot lawmakers putting regulations into place that heavily favor tenants or squatters, whether they had a legal right to be there and traced it all back to spineless legislators. Let me make a point again that I don't think it is a coincidence that Washington DC is overpopulated with attorneys.

People love to protect the dregs until they are squatting in their own backyard. At that point, it is a different ballgame and damn, the neighbors wanted them out. If this was a different neighborhood they would probably have compassion and call me a mean landlord. But you know how people are when something they support is in their back yard? Yep, like the Kennedys and saying "Not in my backyard when it came to wind turbines." Good for the country as long as you don't put those things near us and ruin our view.

The neighbors were getting angry and couldn't believe that I couldn't get these folks out and there was not enough I could do to make the neighbors happy, no matter how much money and time we spent on the situation. We were at the mercy of the courts and legal system. I think we needed some big boys to break some legs, but we don't operate that way. I dream at times that we do!

Yes, we were at the mercy of the courts and our attorney, a legal group that cost me time & money because they didn't have their stuff together. They tend to just go through the motions and lots of stuff falls through the cracks and not just occasionally, which happens all the time with attorney offices. Always some little thing to screw things up but it never ceases to amaze me.

The next big step was how to get these squatters out. Neighbors had stated that they are running amok, fires in the house, gun fire one time, stealing water, electricity, claims of drug sales, cars coming by at all times of the night. This was pretty scary stuff and if I were a neighbor I would be upset also. Calling the local sheriff wasn't doing much good. The neighbors called so much, the Sheriff's office was seemingly tiring of responding and it was obvious that they ignored many of the calls. Not sure I could blame them. As time wore on, I was told that this was a civil case and there wasn't anything they (Sheriff's Office) could do. I assume if they all showed up dead, that eventually the Deputies would have been forced out there to at least pick up the bodies. Even though they had no legal right to be there, and seemingly I had no legal right to evict these folks.

The best I can figure, attorneys sit with politicians. They crouch in corners to create laws and regulations that seemingly care for the good-for-nothing slob, while at the same time ensuring many meaningful billable hours. You just have to love the system lawyers have built for themselves in this country. The laws and regulations supply a steady stream of income during the good times and even more so during the bad times. Then we smartly ship them to Washington D.C. to shape more of our Nations Law. I read that the 2008 administration increased the level of regulation by twenty-five percent (25%) in the first two years in office. Can we all be this gullible? That is just wonderful.

Now in a spat of brilliance with the attorneys, it was decided that a short lease would be better and quicker to get these folks out through the courts. Attorneys are not excited about helping us work around the system in a legal manner (not enough billable hours), but when your own money is at stake, you have to try everything you can. It is my perception that they again are more worried about billing hours, so resolving the situation quickly is not in their favor. So I take a deep breath and put together a month-to-month lease, which we cut short relatively quick, since, surprise, they don't come up with money. These 'squatters' were not rocket scientists as you will see for yourself in the letters we received. Now, I did not ask for a life story from these folks when I took the attorney's advice about doing a month-to-month lease, I was looking for names and social security numbers for background checks to hold in case of trouble and issues. In lieu of basic information, I got these letters detailing some short life summaries. I have no idea what these stories have to do with the basic information I requested. Some folks may feel compassion after reading these notes, but let's not forget, these folks caused the neighbors and the Sheriff endless hours of work and worry, so I was done with bleeding heart sympathy at this point. Eventually the squatters claimed they had one bad apple in the group who caused most of the trouble associated with the yelling, screaming, and idiotic behavior and yes, there were cars everywhere, the occasional gunfire, per the neighbor's reports. Rest assured no work was done on the house by these people and the place was an absolute pigsty, but let's not delay the joy some will get in reading these letters.

This one is from the main character at the house. Put your glasses on to read this stuff. Came to me via pdf fax. No good copies available, so don't complain!

I RAN MR T█████H BUSINESS FOR QUITE SOME TIME BUT I SOON LEARNED HE WAS RIPPING ME OFF BUT TOO THIS DAY IAM SURE HE WOULD ALWAYS GIVE ME A GOOD REFERENCE HERE HIS #425-377-██CONCERT FOR 8 YEARS I OWED MY OWN BUSINESS FOR A YEAR IT WAS CALLED ████ ███ CONCRETE INC. AND AS WE ALL KNOW THE FIRST YEAR IS THE ONE THAT MAKES YOU OR BRAKE YOU WILL IT BROKE ME SEE MY BODY WAS JUST GIVING OUT FROM ALL THE YEARS PRIOR ON CONCRETE A TOTAL OF 20 YEARS IT TARES YOUR BODY UP WHEN I WORKED FOR S██████ I WAS THE SUPERINTENDENT HERE IS A COPY OF MY OLD BUSINESS CARD JUST SO YOU KNOW I AM ON THE UP AND UP. I HAD A CLAIM PRIOR OF OWNING MY BUSINESS WITH ██████ WHEN MY DOCTOR WAS READY FOR MY SECOND SURGERY MY CLAIM HAD EXPIRED SO HE HAD TO REOPEN IT TO DO THE OTHER SHOULDER I WAS BUYING A HOUSE FROM MR T█████, THE OWNER OF ██████R CONCRETE I WAS MAKING 27.5 a hour plus a 20,000 DOLLAR BONUS AT THE END OF THE YEAR SO ONE YR. I PUT DOWN 10,000 ON THIS HOUSE I WAS BUYING FROM HIM HE WAS HOW SHOULD I SAY THIS (SCREWING ME) FOR YEARS MAYBE THAT IS WHY I GOT A 20,000 DOLLAR BONUS AT THE END OF YEAR SEE FOR YEARS HE WAS PAYING ME 117HR. REG AND 15 HOURS OVER TIME HOW CAN THAT BE IN A TWO WEAK PAY PERIOD I HAVE PAY STUBS TO PROVE WHEN I TOOK THEM TO L & I THEY SAID THE AMOUNT IS JUST TO MUCH FOR THEM THAT I WOULD HAVE TO TAKE IT TO A ATTORNEY. WELL THIS IS THE STORY BEHIND THE HOUSE THE CONTRACT WAS ONE PAGE I HAD IT RECORDED AT THE RECORDER OFFICE IN EVERETT SO IT IS ON FILE I WANT TO GET OUT FROM UNDER NEATH HIM TOTAL UNDERSTANDABLE I HAD THREE MORTGAGE CO. THAT WOULD BUY HIM OUT THE HOUSE WAS 189,000 I PUT 10,000 DOWN HAD LIVED THERE FOR THREE YR. I OWED ABOUT 165,000 THREE MORTGAGE CO. AFFORD TO CASH HIM OUT HE SAID NO THAT HE WANTED A EXTRA 20,000 FOR THE BACK LOT WELL THERE WAS NO BACK LOT YOU CAN LOOK AT THE PROPERTY DIMENSION AND SEE THERE IS NO BACK LOT MR RHEO. JUST HAD A LOT MORE EXPERIENCE THEN ME WHEN IT CAME TO THESE KIND OF THING'S SEEING HE OWED ABOUT 25 HOUSE FROM ALL MY HARD WORK IN THE COMPANY ONE MONTH I TURNED IN MY PAPER WORK AND HE TURNED TO ME AND SAID GOOD JOB ███ YOU KNOW WHAT YOU MADE THE CO. THIS MONTH IN PROFIT 86,000 SO SEE HE WAS QUITE PISSED WHEN HE LOST ME AND I STARTED MY OWN BUSINESS AND SO WE DIDN'T KNOW IT THEN BUT NOW WE DO WE SHOULD HAVE GOTTEN HIM FOR real-estate FRAUD WE JUST DIDN'T HAVE KNOW BODY ON OUR SIDE IF THE REAL-ESTATE COMPANY WOULD HAVE BEEN REALLY DOING THERE JOB THEY WOULD HAVE SEEN WHAT WAS GOING ON BUT EVER BODY IS REALLY ONLY AFTER THE ALL MIGHTY $ SO NOBODY SEEN WHAT WAS GOING ON SO WE LOST OUT ON THE HOUSE AND MR T█████O WON AND I RECEIVED A UNLAWFUL DETAINEE WHEN THE CONTRACT WAS A BOGS DEAL IN THE FIRST PLACE. MY WORKMAN COMP. IS 1592.48 EVER TWO WEEKS PLUS WHEN MY SURGERY ARE ALL OVER I WILL RECEIVE A SETTLEMENT TOWARD MY disability WHEN ALL MY SURGERY ARE OVER I WILL RECEIVE A SETTLEMENT. MY BOYS WORK WITH MR R█████A AT THE LAWN CARE SERVICE SO THAT IS MY STORY AGAIN YOU CAN LOOK AT THE ONE PAGE CONTRACT AT THE COUNTY CLERKS OFFICE THE HEADING ON THE CONTRACT IS PURCHASE SALE AGREEMENT SO I LIVED AND LEARNED .

This next one is from his female sidekick. She also sent emails about her pastor standing up for her etc., not sure what got that going either, or who this pastor might be.

I HAVE MY BUSINESS LICENSE I IAM A CARE TAKER AND A HOUSE CLEANER I HAVE ABOUT 10 CLIENTS RIGHT NOW THAT I CLEAN ON A REGULAR BASES SOME I CLEAN ON THRU SOME I CLEAN ON TUES. I STAY VERY BUSY AND MY CLIENTS LOVE ME THEY SAY I CLEAN IN PLACES NOBODY WILL SEE I GET REALLY DETAILED ORIENTED I JUST THINK YOU NEVER KNOW WHERE PEOPLE ARE GOING TO LOOK SO I GET TOOTH BRUSH CLEAN. I HAVE ONE PERSON WORKING WITH ME FROM TIME TO TIME ▄▄▄▄▄▄▄ YES MR. ▄▄▄▄▄ DAUGHTER SHE IS REAL DETAILED AS WELL SHE ALSO CAN TAKE OVER FOR ME IF I HAVE TO GO OUT OF TOWN. I HAVE 20 YR. EXP. IN RETAIL I WORKED FIVE YEARS FOR A CHEVRON STATION AS A MANAGER I ORDERED MERCHANDISE DID BANK DROPS LOADED ATM MY OLD BOSS CAN BE A REFERENCE FOR ME ▄▄▄ AN PHONE NUMBER 425-▄▄▄ THIS IS HIS HOME NUMBER I LOOKED IT ON THE WHITE PAGE ON THE INTERNET I WORKED FOR HIM FOR 5 YEARS I PUT MANY WHERE FROM 110 EVERY TWO WEEKS AND YES MY BOSS PAYED THE RIGHT OVER TIME UNLIKE MR ▄▄▄ I THINK I HAVE FAIR CREDIT I'AM SURE YOU MIGHT SEE SOME CHARGES IN THE PAST BUT LET ME TELL YOU THERE IS ALWAYS TWO SIDE TWO THE STORY YES I HAD SOME CHARGES ON ME BUT I WAS RIDING IN A CAR WHEN IT HAPPENED AND I DID NOT KNOW THAT MY SO CALL FRIENDS DID ANY OF ILLEGAL DRUGS BUT I GOT A SHOCK AND YES I GOT IN TROUBLE FOR THEM SEEING THEY HAD SOMETHING UNDER MY SET WHICH I DI NOT KNOW ABOUT, NEEDLESS TO SAY I DO NOT HANG OUT WITH THEM SEEING I HAD GOT IN THE WORST TROUBLE NOW I KNOW THEY WERE JUST USING ME I'M A LOT MORE CAREFUL TO WHOM I BEFRIEND . REGARDLESS I DO HAVE EXCELLENT CUSTOMER SERVICE SKILLS AND I'M ENJOYING WHAT I DO MY BRING HOME IS ABOUT 2000.00 A MONTH BUT I INTEND TO PUT OUT SOME FLYERS BUT GOOD BUSINESS IS WORD OF MOUTH I AM SURE YOU KNOW . WELL THAT IS THANK YOU FOR BEING PATIENCE WITH ME IN GETTING THESE PAPER TOGETHER. I 'AM QUITE A BUSY LADY I HAVE FOUR CHILDREN WHICH ARE FOR THE MOST PART GROWN BUT IF YOU HAVE KIDS IAM SURE YOU KNOW THEY WILL ALWAYS KEEP YOU HOPPING.!!!

And one of the letters I needed to share, but I would recommend not sharing this brilliance with anyone learning the art of the English language.

I HAVE RUNNING MY BUSINESS FOR THREE YEARS AND LIKE WHAT I DO WE ARE VERY SUCCESSFUL NOW I HAVE SEVERELY CLIENTS AND WE ARE CALLED NW LAWN CARE WE ARE INTENDING TO GET INC. SEEING MY CUSTOMER LIST IS GETTING SO BIG. MY AVERAGE BRINGS HOME IN A MONTH IS CLOSE TO 5000. BUT SEEING WE ARE IN THE COLDER WEATHER IT HAS DROPPED A LITTLE ABOUT 3000. STILL NOT BAD IF I SAY SO MY SELF. I HAVE OWED MANY HOUSES IN DETROIT THAT IS WERE I AM FROM IN FACT I STILL OWEN A HOUSE RIGHT NOW SO IF NEEDS BE I COULD TAKE A LOAN OUT ON THAT. WE HAVE ALL DISCUSSED THIS ISSUE AND WE CAN COME UP WITH A 5000.00 DEPOSIT ALL THE PEOPLE ON THIS LIST MAKE A INCOME. I DON'T KNOW WHAT YOU HAVE HEARD FROM THE MR. ████████S OR NEIGHBOR'S OR WHOEVER OR WHATEVER BUT WE ARE ALL HARD WORKING PEOPLE THAT ARE INTERESTED IN PURCHASING THIS HOUSE WE HAVE PUT A LOT OF TIME AND EFFORT INTO IT THINKING IT WAS ALREADY ON A CONTRACT BUT WE SOON FOUND OUT WRONG WE WENT DOWN TO PAY THE ELECTRIC BILL AND THEY SAID WE COULD NOT? WE WENT DOWN TO PAY THE WATER BILL AND THEY SAID WE COULD NOT AND STILL WE WANTED TO STAY BECAUSE WE THOUGHT THERE WAS A CONTRACT WORKED OUT WE ARE AT THIS TIME RUNNING ON A GENERATOR AND BRING WATER INTO THE HOUSE OUR SELVES WE GO OVER TO FAMILY AND TAKE OUR SHOWERS WE USE PROPANE HEAT AND ARE STILL WORKING ON THE HOUSE AS MUCH AS WE CAN WE HAVE CLEANED THIS PLACE UP TIMELESSLY WE HAVE PAINTED THE BASEMENT AND THE ENTIRE WE HAVE CLEANED THE YARD UP WASHED WINDOWS WE ALL HAVE PUT A LOT OF TIME AND MONEY AND OUR LOVE INTO THIS HOUSE SO GOING FORWARD HERE IS THE PEOPLE WE WANT ON THE CONTRACT.OUR INTENTION IS TO ALL OF US LIVE HERE FOR A WHILE AND THEN TAKE A LOAN OUT FOR ONE OF US TO PUT DOWN ON ANOTHER HOUSE AFTER ABOUT A YEAR OR MORE WE FIGURED THAT WOULD BUT MAYBE ENOUGH TIME WE ALL HOPE AND PRAY WE CAN KEEP THIS HOUSE SEEING WE HAVE PUT SO MUCH EFFORT INTO IT SO HERE ARE THE OTHER PEOPLE INVOLVED.

I know, I know, I shouldn't mock those who cannot read or write very well, which I am not an expert in, but I had to crack up. They paint themselves with this canvas of what hard working folks they are; down on their luck and all that, however, the reality is totally different than what they portray. Check out the sheriff reports. Plus, there is no obligation for our families to provide for all these folks, regardless of how down on their luck they might be, or pretend to be.

The stress from the problem occupants of this property caused from 2007 to 2010 is ridiculous. It did help us determine that we wanted nothing to do with the State of Washington. It was, and is, too risky to have a multitude of assets there in residential property. It is just too difficult to get things done, whether it is dealing with the justice system and evictions or assistance in stopping crimes against our property and other people (neighbors). It is just not worth the risk.

WASHINGTON STATE: THE FINALE

After various contacts with the neighbors, to include a few yelling matches letting them know I can only get results based on the dollars we spend with the attorneys and the many sheriff calls I made, we did start to make some progress. I made calls to check on children seen in the property and other various instances of alleged crime that neighbors believed they were witnessing. After some time, we finally got an eviction order. But know this, the squatters may not write well, but they knew when to put something in front of the courts to delay an eviction. I had to agree to forgo chasing them down for the near $8,000.00, that's eight thousand dollars that it cost for the eviction alone. Totally absurd and further proof of a broken legal system in my opinion!

On the day the sheriff came, we had our representative there to witness the squatters move most of their trash outside. What didn't help us was that one of the deputies seemed to get special giggles from telling these lower than life individuals that they didn't have to move it themselves and the owner was required by law to move the stuff out and into storage. Yea, thanks for the legal advice Deputy Do Right. Shut up. At least the other Deputy was apparently cool about it and hustled these folks along.

Can you believe a system that requires the family that owns a home, where squatters have moved in and refuse to pay rent, have to pay to move the unlawful tenants out AND store their belongings? Come on, that is just jacked up, no matter how you explain it. The law should let us throw it in the front yard and roast marshmallows on a bonfire with the property.

These illegal residents did eventually get everything out and we agreed, how nice of us, to give them 72 hours to remove the rest/trash from the yard etc. We then proceeded to board up the house, shut it down, and end of the story, right? No way.

Immediately after moving these folks out of the property, I start getting calls from the neighbors saying these sweet down on their luck squatters were breaking into the house yet again. People, please, give it up please! Calling the sheriff did no good. Boarding it up again did no good. These folks were like roaches coming out when the lights went off. They just found their way back to the house and would break in at night. To do what, I wasn't sure. I had to hire a security firm to patrol the property. $4,000 in security costs and we think they finally gave it up. When the rehabilitation contractor gets on site, literally dumping more of our dollars, he informs us of little places where they were growing weed and doing drugs along with needles strewn everywhere. What a wonderful experience I have in this business. Dealing with such nice people!

Yes, they needed the protection of the system in order to smoke weed and do whatever sort of drugs they were into. We created such an intrusion into their lives to evict them. They had weed to smoke and needles to use in that house. How dare we interrupt these free-loaders from using drugs and leaching off of us! I was waiting for someone to call me and say it was our responsibility to take care of them. Seriously, I kid you not, I was deathly afraid this is how it might play out, no matter how absurd it might seem.

What a pain. I do have to note that the best service I seemed to get from the sheriff was when I asked if anyone worked off duty for security. Damn! Bang, Pow! That question got me a phone number and an e-mail, as well as a person to speak with right away. I got pricing and information galore. Try getting that service with a complaint as a Joe-Schmo citizen not paying extra for public service.

Overall I have to give credit to the neighbors for watching the house like a hawk, with binoculars and a microphone I was told at one point. The poor neighbor who I talked to the majority of the time called scared to death one time after the eviction when she ran into them seemingly trespassing again and called the sheriff. She was fearful they would come visit her home, since they saw her. I felt so bad for her having to live in fear like that. I think she is thinking twice about her voting habits now when it comes to people who make the laws. (*We had talked politics and we were on different sides of the fence it seems*) She might lean more to the conservative side now, or so I would hope. But give it time and I'm sure she will forget about that fear and get back to her old self.

So three years later, with enormous financial loss we finally get the home back to make repairs and either rent or sell. Hopefully this is just an amusing memory for most of the neighbors as we move forward to get this house in the hands of a decent family. We did finally finish cleaning up the property after dropping another one hundred thousand dollars into the house. Check that! $100K plus! Gotta love this country. We couldn't sell the property during this economic downturn, so we resorted to renting it out with hopes of selling it a few years down the road. It is a sweet house now with a beautiful deck and an indoor pool on a great piece of land. But it is also a house with considerable history. All I want to hear at this point from that property is crickets chirping or children playing. No gunshots or screaming please. And let's forgo the piles of excrement reeking from the property, or using the real estate as a parking lot. Fingers crossed!!

PENNSYLVANIA: LUXURY LIVING AT NO COST

In September 2010, I had to drag my broken down body off to the airport to fly to Pennsylvania to check on some problem properties. It was also a good opportunity to check in on borrowers and renters in the surrounding area. We were in a few foreclosure proceedings with some folks and it is good to put eyes on the properties now and then.

One property that I visited was a home that we had been renting to a former borrower who proceeded to trash the property after we extended him our helping hands. This was in tandem with yet another former borrower, who we allowed to rent back from us after foreclosure for a period of eight months. This method, in my opinion, allows the borrowers to get their finances and personal situation in order before they had to move. The mess both of these borrowers-turned-renters had left was disgusting and disappointing. The chaos they left in the wake of their departures was justification for me to contact another family member in the loan investment to fly in and meet me there. It was my hope that his construction experience would be helpful to me in evaluating the properties for disposition, plus having another set of eyes see what I see and smell helps the investment team realize I'm not making this stuff up.

I knew that this was going to be a good experience for him to see what I what I had to deal with on a consistent basis. Our first stop was a house where the borrower owed us over five hundred thousand dollars ($500K) and never made a payment on the loan. You read that right: NEVER MADE A PAYMENT is correct. Not a typo. He worked full time, had a huge home in a beautiful area and was screwing with us at every turn. He got the loan in 2007, proceeded to pay off his other legal obligations, and then began incurring new debt with us. Total loser! Better yet, just another jerk.

He was employed with a good job, but the records show that he didn't pay anyone anywhere in the state when it came to debts. Yea, yea, I know, how & why did someone lend him money? I don't know anymore, but it was sure easy to get refinanced back then.

We gathered that this guy may have been a 'tweaker' (that means a 'Meth addict'...I guess I did learn something else from the Washington State losers). Our local agent thought he was strung out during the times he made contact with him about the home. But who knows? I just think he was just lowlife scum who constantly abused the system and the system protected him along the way. I cannot recall how many attorneys he went through, or how many bankruptcy filings he had. This one was personal to us, there was lots of money in that house, and we weren't getting a dime off of it. In fact, this home was costing us thousands a year to carry while this loser gets to live in for free. This was seemingly typical of our society at this point.

The disappointment and frustration surrounded this place. It would rear its ugly head a few times, such as when our local attorney, erred with filing paperwork in the first foreclosure sale right out the chute. This gave the borrower time to gather himself and his ammunition, and then we battled for years. Even sadder was the fact that the attorney e-mailed us that it was their error and they would make it right. Can you guess if they did? No, they didn't make it right. Don't expect that ever from a legal office. EVER! We had to continue our legal battle even after we finally got the home back after a 2009 Foreclosure sale. It took us up to late August 2010 to evict this borrower, turned squatter. He was in this home all that time for free although we legally OWNED THE HOME. We had to call the Law when we visited the property to inspect and noticed he was chipping away at the pool and continued to chip away at it until we finally got him out. Nothing we could do but wait. He was an expert at filing bankruptcy (BK) and the eviction process was no different. The courts would immediately delay until we could provide a legal filing showing the history before we could get the eviction rolling again. Even though the BK was vacated, it took us another few months to get another eviction date. When I finally got the order of eviction, I had to convince the local Deputy to actually evict him in a timely manner. The Deputy felt bad for him and wanted to give him another 6 weeks since the tenant had complained to him that he was taken advantage of in the loan process through predatory practices, oh shut up!!!…ARGH!! You had no idea how I hated hearing the words from Deputy Dog and had to remain calm with him. #1 the whole scenario was absolute bs and #2 the Deputy is there to enforce the law, not interpret it, completely ridiculous and out of line.

Eventually, the Deputy came to understand this guy was scum and the scum didn't even give us the benefit of watching him get out. He left and vacated the night before the eviction. We did hear the Deputy checked his record and found he owed child support, scammed his mother, etc., so he felt good about kicking him out. Thanks!

The following are some pictures of the house he lived in over 3 years WITHOUT MAKING ONE SINGLE PAYMENT but took out considerable sums of cash in the refinance. Even with all this, the system has laws to protect him, regardless. Not sure why anyone would even consider lending money for a house purchase with the laws stacked against the lender.

Decent home…from the outside!

Lovely green water with chipped tile

Makes you want to jump right in!!

Empty shed, could be useful. Bodies in there ya think?

More pool damage

Random ceiling holes.   No water damage, just a hole!

Kitchen, not too bad, right after new cabinets.

Painted hardwood... Who paints hardwood floors?

Do we need to be cleaned?

More damage.

Thanks for the treasure of trash

Filthy bathrooms, dingy walls and busted up rooms. This Pennsylvania Prince never took care of the palace during his reign. Every place we have had to foreclose on with a pool has been a mess and seriously, who paints a hardwood floor? Did you see that picture?

You would think that someone not paying for that long would have put some of the money into the property to enjoy and relax. Nope. They do what most do, they let the property lie in disrepair and deteriorate further and further until the place is almost unlivable or, as in this case, was unlivable. We listed the property for sale in 2010 and struggled to sell it sometime in 2011 I believe. We did find out that in the interim our old loser borrower may serve prison time. It seems he perpetrated a scam to rob his elderly mother of all her savings. As I write this, the local DA contacted me for an interview. I found out that he had installed himself with Power of Attorney over his mother's finances and took out thousands of dollars for cars and vacations along with anything else he could get his hands on, oh, except paying the mortgage. The Sergeant working the case was positive he would be thrown in jail. I hope he spends eternity in there. I understand his mother was now in a county home at the taxpayer expense also. Poor woman, so sorry she had such a scum bag for a son. Who does that to their mother? Well the same guy that screwed us. Many of these folks don't really care who they hurt or basically steal from. Truly disheartening, and the saddest part of this is that we still hear discussion every week from DC about helping people like this with our hard earned money.

So for those of you thinking this guy was taken in through predatory lending practices, you can all kiss my butt.

PENNSYLVANIA: POTENTIAL POSITIVE

Our second stop in PA was to a home that was so beautiful inside. There were antiques that would take your breath away. This property was in need of some work, but we were attempting to work a deal to avoid foreclosure with the borrower and the borrower's attorney. We weren't getting a payment each month, but we would get payments fairly regularly and we wanted to give them time to work something out. They were paying and living up to their end of the bargain at the time and we respected that, so we continued to work something out so that they could pay us off in a year without us having to impose tough constraints on them. They were rebuilding the outside deck and applying improvements in accordance with the codes and requirements befitting a home of that age and time in history. Seemingly, they were people that actually cared for the property and were sincere in their efforts. We had hoped that this would be a highlight for us down the road and in coming years when it was off our books. That dream disappeared quickly when we tried to negotiate a new agreement with them, an agreement in their favor! They fell off the radar, and stopped paying in early 2011. Without being able to contact them personally or through their lawyer, we eventually gave up and initiated foreclosure actions, which was very disheartening to say the least. Not only did we believe we finally had borrowers who had some morale fiber and wanted to better their situation, we had hoped they would pay us off and be on their way to better things. Besides, it was a very expensive house to be financing from our end with over $650K owed us. This one hurt.

Screech, wait!!!! Hit the brakes. These folks eventually came back to us, worked a deal and guess what? They actually sent in some checks!! Not kidding. Pray they keep moving in this direction! Now, for this property, I surely hope they sell the property this year and pay off many debts besides ours.

Hit the brakes again. One payment and back to the foreclosure process. Endless cycle. I should not have stopped the foreclosure first time around, since I lose months if not years, but once you accept a payment during a foreclosure, you have to cancel it legally. Home is in foreclosure as of this 2nd edition writing. No income for us for years on close to ¾ of a millions dollars, while this borrower uses the property free to run his business and live upstairs. Sad times for lenders in my mind.

PENNSYLVANIA: GOT TO SEE IT TO BELIEVE IT

My next action adventure along the trails of PA had no positive moments at all. This was a property we took in foreclosure in 2009 and cut a cheap six month deal that extended to eight months for a borrower who had now become our renter. I was told that her husband had passed away so we wanted to help make a tough situation a little easier. She had an attorney help her at first pro bono, but he quietly bowed out early on and we soon found out why. We had decided to give her some time to gather herself instead of just showing her the door. What I didn't know was the atmosphere which they lived.

This was a property where they owed us in the $190K range. When we finally got the home back, we determined that we would have to sell this off as a scrapeoff; it was in such poor condition. The home had literally deteriorated, which was depressing, since at one time it was a nice home and it was in a nice neighborhood. This was simply another kick in the butt for us to deal with and it was disgusting to say the least. Words and pictures cannot describe how I felt, and what I smelt, when I walked into the place. It overwhelmed me and smelled like animal and human urinepiss and feces. Plus, as an extra bonus of the visit, I was severely flea bitten when I finished visiting the home (*using the word home loosely*). As an added bonus item we had to deal with, the old borrower and now renter, wanted some of their deposit back. I thought to myself, they want money back and this place will cost over $4,000 just to clean up the mess they left behind and then sell as a trash pit for a huge loss.

This was not anywhere near "broom clean condition" per the lease. Unless the broom she was using had hammers attached to it and a special pump to shoot out poop and urine every 3-4 inches. Even though I said pictures don't provide the real story, since the smell and 360-view is missing, I will show some pictures anyhow. Why not share the fun.

First I will lead off with a picture of my flea bites. They drove me crazy! Cannot scrub enough!! @#&$^%@#(&*^%(*&^!!!!!!!!!!!!!!   Peroxide!! Showering constantly. Arghhhhhhh!!!

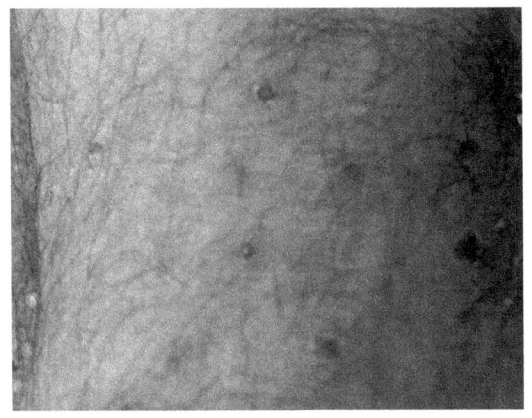

PA flea bites. Little bums!!

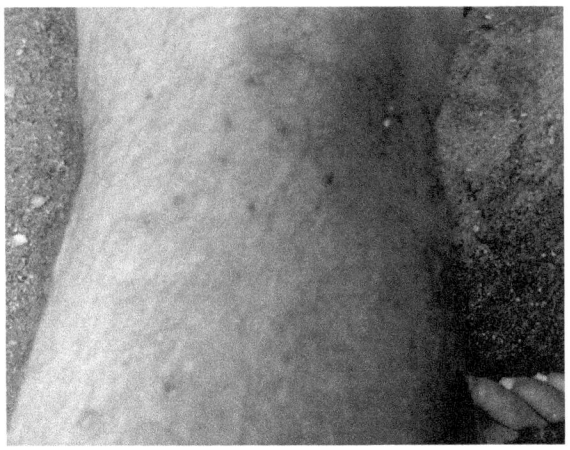

Those are truly nasty little SOBS!!

I hated that I went in there to check this place out; I still shudder when I think about this nightmare. I loaded myself up with hydrogen peroxide and calamine lotion after I left this property. The whole time I was thinking that I didn't sign up for this.

Now for the beautiful well-kept interior and exterior of the property.

Mmmm, warm and cozy

Just the right amount of clutter.

Where did I put the ice cream scooper?

I think the maids must've just left.

The smell in here was not good. I looked for the body, seriously!

Nicely kept backyard, don't you think?

Sort of like a Resort jungle cruise in that pool.

Nice place for a grill and cabana.

More of that PA State green water.

Minor upkeep issues

Somewhere in the house?

I think they were teachers, I see a book!

This place was just an absolute pigsty. In the appraisal in 2007 the house looked great, it only took them 2-3 years to totally ruin this home. What gets into people, or doesn't get into people to clean? These people were also employed.

But I assume someone loves them, cuz I sure as heck think they are trash-hoarding bums who just wanted more and more from someone or anyone. Some people in this country can be downright disgusting. One thing that gets me is that this person had grown children. I would think you would check in on your parents now and then, just to make sure they were ok. Help them clean up maybe, don't you think? Do some minor maintenance on the home. What is wrong with our society? Do children no longer come to the rescue of their aging parents? They should never let them live like this. The smell of human and animal waste (the urine!) was overwhelming. There was even a room where some large bird lived, not caged, with droppings evident everywhere.

To make matters worse this was such a good looking neighborhood. The neighbors will be relieved to see us out there draining the mosquito pool, ripping up the rotted deck and cleaning the place out. This was just way too expensive to refurbish with all the apparent problems with the property. You do walk away wondering what happened, how things can go so bad in the span of three years. In these years they allowed the property to deteriorate, and who knows what happened to the refinance money? We will never know. People take cash and say they want to make improvements to their home, but then they never get around to it, or it was never their intention in the first place, and the money slowly evaporates. Someone got the benefit of that house equity, maybe a cruise company, the local bar, local drug dealer? Maybe they had a sweet ride? We will just never know.

PENNSYLVANIA: MORE DISPAIR, DISAPPOINTMENT, AND DISMAY

The worst and most depressing stop was in the Philly area. It was a large row-house, townhouse, brownstone or whatever they call it there. This was a case where the borrower gave us the deed back instead of facing foreclosure, and then he rented the property back from us at a fairly inexpensive rental rate. We gave him an option to purchase at that amount which was owed. Of course this never happened. The borrower disappeared on us after missing many of the rental payments, which was actually expected. Heck they didn't pay the mortgage, so why expect they would pay the rent?

I think there is some art in it nowadays. I find it amazing that people seemingly plan to only stay a short period of time in a home and not pay, then just keep moving around. I am sure that our group is not the first or last to deal with the same borrower in the same situation.

Back to the next homestead, this was also a pigsty. There were holes in roof, small horse troughs filled with water, and some of that same urine smell I encountered at the previous PA Palace. No operational bathroom, kitchen tore up, walls tore down. Just sad and we had $200K invested in this property through yet another borrower who had taken out cash in a refinance to work on the property. I have to gather that money also went up in smoke, someone's nose or into cars, vacations, but guaranteed not the house. Do you wonder why after a while you become jaded and numb to dealing with such disgusting situations?

Everywhere we turn; there are people screwing us over, people who want something for free; people always looking for a bailout without giving anything to anyone else; hand out, palm up. That is the behavior this country coddles and approves of as appropriate and acceptable.

Well folks, I am completely done dealing with that mentality, it is emotionally and physically exhausting. Plus, it is unfair to those that do the right thing, those that are trying to work with us, those that are making an effort every day to meet not only their obligation to us, but their other commitments as well. But I repeat, we live in a society where we bend over backwards to bail those folks out and guess who loses America? Yep, the ones who bust their butts, probably folks just like you. Yes, we do.

Check out the next line up of photos.

Another nicely kept room.

Sweet bathroom!! No wall from my side.

What happened to the bathroom wall? Picture was taken from the hallway.

Second bathroom, unfinished I guess.

Kitchen is cozy.

1 Upstairs room, with water bucket.

More water buckets.

At the time of our visit we were unsure what we would do with the property. There were similar properties in the neighborhood. It seems the neighborhood got rundown from people not taking care of what could have been a beautiful place. No one seemed to care. We ended up taking a financial kick in the pants and just sold it, as is, for a small amount of money, nothing near what we paid in, it was a lose-lose all around for us.

The rest of the Pennsylvania trip was pretty uneventful. It involved my knocking on doors so folks knew we could reach out and touch them.

And you know what I learned? People are not used to the lender, the accounts payable guy, receivables guy, the vice president and minister of all things in the company showing up at their door in a rental car and shorts and being able to reach out and touch you. Hi there, it's just me!!!!

Hey folks, it's all we have to offer. We are the epitome of the small business. It was me knocking on doors. Just me! I tended to get a lot of calls while driving around the areas, after these folks would freak out when they would see a card from the lender on their door. 'Oh no! What is wrong? What did I do?' In our case it is nice to tell folks we are just visiting, staying in touch, inspecting properties, this is all. It's really good for us to see the properties in person, instead of hearing about the condition from local agents, or checking the old appraisal.

PENNSYLVANIA: THE REST OF THE STORY

It was especially pleasant to finally see the home of a guy in Philly who had befriended me and I gave him opportunity to make it right with us. Time and time again I would do this, until I tired of it. We delayed the inevitable for so long, and eventually, you realize they are just screwing with you yet again.

This guy had a very nice place with great value and a good amount of equity. He wanted me to forgive most of his debt interest at a minimum. Reality was he needed to just sell the home and pay us off. We had incurred substantial costs on the property and he needed to live up to his end of the bargain. We also found out his family has some nice upscale restaurants just down the street from the house. We even ate there. Seems we should have gotten a discount, because I am guessing that is where much of the equity money from the house ended up. People have no qualms about using our money for their business ventures and then cry and whine when payment is due. Bums!

We continue to battle this guy and this property. I refused to falsify payment records so he could get a refinance and he complained to the courts. I am sure he didn't tell them why I refused to give him payment records showing him as performing. Crazy. Then months later he wanted us to take about a $80,000.00 hair cut on the property. I told them it wasn't going to happen. 3 years in and I offer him $15,000.00 and a new 1 year balloon and promise to not fight foreclosure if he misses payments and months later, not a peep. Go figure.

During the trip in PA, I actually found most of the homes we held the loans against were in good condition. I even got to see the home of the borrower who rotated in and out of foreclosure and would reinstate every 3-4 months. It was an investment property for him and he was actually trying to sell the property he used as a rental. It will be good to quit chasing these folks and get them off our books someday. This one was to be at foreclosure sale during November 2012, but hurricane sandy delayed this and we are still waiting.

This will allow us to focus on our good performers and see if we can find something to help them refinance, then everyone goes on their own merry way in the end.

Overall my Pennsylvania trip was helpful and entertaining and I did get to see different parts of the country. You can get a sense of folks by seeing a house right in front of you, with your own eyes (and nose), from the porch or stoop. Is the door off the hinges? Are there trash bags strewn everywhere. Is it freshly painted? Overall you try to find out if they do care about the property and this can give you an idea of whether you end up in a fight or if they will go quietly.

We did find a property in what I consider a very sweet location, although this one was in foreclosure. It had plenty of nice acreage, a new fifth wheel on a large expanse of blacktop and this long kick-butt driveway that was lined by beautiful trees. I struggled to communicate with them, since they never answered my calls, e-mails or letters. I had no clue what was happening with this place, but they had equity in the home and in my firm opinion, they needed to sell and regroup after they give us our money back. Not sure what they did with the money either. This one went to sale in April of 2011, one year after working the foreclosure.

The stories never end really in this business and I am one guy who will be so relieved when we get out after real estate finally turns around. So, what is our lesson as a country? The lesson is to not lend money to folks with poor credit and horrendous spending habits, period. The upside of this economic downturn is folks who shouldn't have credit, won't be able to get it anymore, or so I think. This tightening up of credit for poor performers should have been done years ago. Eventually things will improve and our lawyer/politicians will again get up on their high horse and pressure folks to lend to those in the area below the gray area. Just wait for it. And if you're not here when it happens, don't worry, your children will be, or their children. We need to understand our financial history as much as our geographical history.

SUPER LAWERS: ALL FOR ONE AND ONE FOR THEMSELF!!

You know what I am really tired of? What is it that just fries me and pisses me off? Or, as my friend says, what makes me want to scratch my jock itch with a rabid porcupine? Well, of course, it is these wonderful pro-bono, justice-center, group-hug, gonna help you against the big bad lender …LAWYERS. Enough already!

I have to deal with these clowns who defend people like those who break into homes and then squat in them; People who are making themselves at home for free; The lawyers jump in with so much so-called compassion and are supposedly defending the downtrodden and people in despair. Before this, I really thought there was a need for the so-called help, but now I realize that they all have a mission and a selfish mission really. It brings these so-called do-gooders clients or potential lawsuits to bulk up their wallets (again with our money). No, there is no overriding generosity here or some mission to provide others goodwill. Hell, they defend folks similar to criminal lawyers, regardless if the person in front of them is in the right or wrong, which their client is just not paying so it would be the latter. We all know there is a judicial process in this beautiful country, but as a lawyer friend of mine said so accurately, "The legal system is harder on the innocent than the guilty." We bend over backwards for the guilty in this country.

You can kill 12 people and they look for ways to redeem you. Oh, poor baby, someone ridiculed him for wearing black lipstick with a black trench coat and black eyeliner to high school in the summer. Good God people, if a boy wears that, he does it for attention and then doesn't like the attention he gets and shoots people; poor baby? Or the guys who supposedly have a rough childhood so it is ok to steal and beat people, and then they pout in a jailhouse picture so people oooh and ahh like they are some baby in a newborn nursery. Poor baby, no one loved him, so no wonder he hurt so many people. Let's all give him a hug, free housing, money, whatever he wants so he can get out and do it again. How about those who refuse to pay their bills? Oh, how unfair. Do you want to hear what they did with the cash these folks took out of the house? No, that is not important. They probably needed that vacation, the drugs, or that shiny new car, doesn't matter. Not fair that you ask them to pay it back, look at them, sunken eyes, depression, so don't feel bad. Shouldn't you forgive them and just move on? Oh, poor babies.

I had the distinct pleasure of trying to work with legal counsel in Washington State. Dum duh duh...here the justice league came to the rescue. Here's the story. I have this borrower who in July of 2010 was 16 months down on a loan that was 36 months old after she had refinanced and took cash out for who knows what. As of this update add another 24 months of no payments. Yes, 40 months down and I don't have the property yet. We, the big bad lender, were doing nothing but trying to work with this person for 2 years, to cut them some slack, find a way to help them repair their credit, anything but take the house. We are the little people also, but apparently we don't count when we are a small business. The years 2009 thru 2012, and who knows for how much longer, was not a time for our business to make money. Not a profitable business when no one wants to pay or demands you forgive their debt, or just asks you to give them the home at no cost. I am certainly not a rich man, but I do everything I can to try and help these folks. As I have said before, I try to get those homeowners who have equity to sell their homes to recoup this equity. They could live off of this equity until they recover from whatever turmoil might be causing them to not pay us, etc. So many are just stubborn and refuse to do this.

Anyhow, back to this story. This certain borrower was delinquent as are most in our pool of loans. I wanted to give them a year to recover, so in 2009 I cut their payment by 30%. Healthy cut, don't you think? Well, it doesn't help them since they immediately start missing those payments to us also. It was early in my on the ground training as a lender representative and I honestly thought this would help people. I have since learned otherwise. This was my first clue that it doesn't matter, these folks cannot afford the home. But wait… I have not given up on them. I send letters about them being aggressive to look for help, credit repair, everything I can do and then in the year 2010 I offer them a chance to extend the forbearance agreement and give them the options: deed-in-lieu, foreclosure, etc. and even yes, please sell the home to recover your equity and find affordable living arrangements.

It is fine and dandy that people are attached to the old homestead, but please don't push your financial troubles on to us and ask that we support your home. Before I cut a new agreement I knew I needed a hammer to let them know this was serious. So for the 2010 agreement we threw in a caveat about signing over a warranty deed if they defaulted and tried to convey to them this was serious. So here we were with this new agreement where we would only accept this forbearance if they signed a warranty deed that we could record in a default. I learned after time that people only seem to respond to serious consequences and straight-forward results that they will lose their home, or so I thought. It seemed fair to me, after the two years we hung on, these folks were seriously delinquent and not doing anything. So when they started to get further behind in 2010 I called, sent letters and even had a contact in Washington State personally knock on the door. The final conclusion was obvious. They just couldn't afford the home. Even though I suggested they sell it themselves to recover any equity that might be left, they never listed it and obviously were not planning on it. After a while, you sense they are calling your bluff, if it was a bluff. It's not a bluff anymore.

I finally got tired of not getting results from my efforts to help, so I sent the deed into recording at the county. I also had our guy on the ground talk to them and offer them money to help them move. They were on board with this initially.

It must have been just after this they called the law firm of FJLS, the Free Junior League of Superheroes. (Music plays here). Ok, if I wanted to get out of my obligation with a firm that I had said thank you to so many times for giving me a break and forestalling the obvious and I was still not paying them, yea, I would plead ignorance and whatever else and then call them bad guys (that's us, the bad guys, I mean I wear black now and then so why not?). Would I say they cheated me? I guess yes for them, it was the obvious thing to do. Lie and do whatever it takes to now screw the guys who gave you a break for 2 years. About then the legal crime-stopping circus came to town with the Justice Minor league, or something like that. We got news that they were waiting for disability checks from us? Say what!? Never heard this before now, and I have no concept of what this means, nor do I care.

How about the fact we are waiting for our mortgage checks for over 2 years. I assume this means that they want me to delay this again for 2 years. Fat chance people, fat chance!

As you can tell from reading this book, I was really tired of the excuses and people playing on our emotions. Emotions that after a while disappear since you hear the same stories so many times over and over again. You tend to not believe anything you hear, and if something is true, it is at a point that it doesn't matter any longer. We cannot afford ills and pains from everyone who is 'down on their luck,' or so they say. Now, if you think we are lame for not forestalling this even further, you can find us and buy the loan from us, and then work with these folks at your pleasure and get your game on feeling groovy while languishing for years without any real sign of getting your money back. Please be my guest…really, please? It's all fun and games, and nonsense news stories, until it is your hard earned money folks. In a way, it actually is your money in the long run.

Okay, so that is fine, you have problems for 1-2-3 years, but again, please quit asking us, our small group, and others to support your problems with their hard-earned money. I feel the pain too, but make smart decisions. This happened to you, not us. Is that cold, yes, but I have an obligation to look out for my family and my interests, not yours. Again I say to those who sneer at us, we will sell you any amount of loans you want and then you can manage them, be a great humanitarian, and deal with the troubles of others, get that lump in your throat and that hole in your wallet. Come play in our game, and then comment on how you can be MVP.

Is it right that people think they can spread their misfortune onto others to absorb and then say we have no compassion? Hell we have compassion; we have compassion for our families and our friends in need. Come on people, we are just strung pretty thin with balancing our compassion and other's finances, and we just don't want to pay for it every day for everyone's empathetic needs. Our families are trying to make this business operate, not just donate homes. Yes, I know, some of you folks love these legal firms and want them to go forth in their fight to strangle small American firms like us. Bad company making money, bad bad bad, because it's not my money. Put every small business on the bread line, they deserve that, bad company. Shut up and get over it already.

In 2012 I saw a video on line at one of the political conventions with the commentator asking folks if we should "ban profits"? This was so stupid it was funny and time after time, people at this convention agreed, yes, we should ban profits. How stupid are we?

Anyhow, this Captain American lawyer didn't return my calls but instead sent letters to our attorney that said, *the borrower doesn't remember signing any of that stuff, and we shouldn't take their home with that much equity, and that I coerced them, blah blah* ...and that apparently I should listen to counsel about what our objectives are meant to accomplish. Give me a break. They cite some law saying it may be immoral or illegal, *not fair*, or whatever to get the deed that way in this state, great way to find this out. So now it's a morality determination to NOT pay your debt? Well, after speaking with our attorney we decide to rescind the deed and go through the foreclosure and give her a chance to sell it herself and capture her equity.

What the heck I thought at this point. Let's just do this for expediency and value. It's cheaper to push the foreclosure than fight the deed issue. Do I think she will sell the home even though Captain America says she will with more time? Nope. I checked the listings and home was not up for sale. The last communiqué to us was taking a short sale on the home or give them a real low interest rate. Not interested at all in dealing with folks who do not honor obligations. They will wait for the day of the foreclosure sale and come up with some whining excuse etc., but at this point, after I have spent two years calling, writing and trying to tell them to make a smart decision, pay their bills, there will be no more deals cut. They actually did what everyone else does.

They didn't sell the home but filed bankruptcy to forestall the foreclosure, yet again. This will eventually take another year and I gather they will call us the day before the foreclosure sale and ask us for some ridiculous help. These free lawyers need to understand that we will not cut deals or negotiate with people who do not honor their word, and in fact lie through their teeth that we are fraudulent. After all the lying and stabbing us in the back, they want me to again try and negotiate a deal, which is just not going to happen. The last story we got was that this lady had a roommate who was behind on rent and they couldn't make a payment right now to catch anything up since they were traveling in Europe. Oh God, say it ain't so! Taking a European trip while they are in foreclosure and filing bankruptcy, you have to love this country. They are probably collecting food stamps at the same time. I wonder if you can exchange them for Euro-dollars or food stamps. Ha, not so funny. The last deal was we would agree to delay and they would vacate on a specific date. Didn't happen and we had to go back to the courts to evict them and process through the whole legal process. They didn't lie to us once, twice or even three times, they lie until they get called on it and kicked out. Simple legal process. Lame, just lame.

Business Rule: Do not negotiate more deals with people who you know DO NOT HONOR their word or commitment. It never ends up good, ever. Now don't say I didn't warn you.

Talking to these Captain America legal types is truly educational and entertaining at the same time. I am sure there are a few good ones out there who also try and educate their clients in finances and life and scold them to not get too deep into this sort of situation ever again, but, they haven't called me yet.

They can be like the billboard lawyers who carry the sword for these people and promise them that they can negotiate new loan mods, save the home and all sorts of other hollow promises. These lawyers are dirty in my opinion. Just like the private attorneys who advertise to save homes and take a monthly stipend from the borrowers with the same hollow promises of saving their homes. They take what should be the mortgage money, giving folks the impression not paying their debt is o.k. This will be stuck in the system for years; all the while the legal boys will be collecting monthly payments to pad their pockets, occasionally filing a bogus boilerplate document to delay the investable a few more months to collect a few more months of legal fees. Just stop paying the attorneys and see what happens, they disappear clean out of sight. These are the same jerks that give us the evil eye in a deposition about how bad we are, even though we haven't been paid in 2-3 years, but they skip out day ONE on people once they don't get their bills paid. They are jackals, yes indeed. Heed caution of these filthy jackal pigs robbing the borrowers blind under this ruse of being these super lawyers and helping save their home.

They find people, many struggling, and fill them with false hope and just ring up a monthly revenue stream for years on end. One can make pretty good bank doing that. All these lawyers push for new loans when the fact is, the vast majority of lenders cannot, and will not, afford a 0% loan and these legal beagles know this. We get our money at a much higher percentage than what they want us to offer. Even though we communicate this to borrowers and their lawyers, they still want us to give it back at some ridiculous loan rate with a huge loss of cash to us. Listen out there: Maybe Bank of America can absorb these huge losses (maybe, but doubtful), but little folks cannot and should not. Somewhere that should click in their little greased heads that it won't fly. It got to a point that I had to make it clear to our attorneys that like the US with foreign entities, there would be NO MORE NEGOTIATIONS! We needed to just tell them we wanted full reinstatement or deed the home to us, period.

By the time I sent something to foreclosure, I had spent months, and usually years, working with the people with no real results. It became just a waste of time to continue negotiations and mediations. Of course the real jerks petition the court for a deposition and ask you mundane questions to drag the process out even further, which is absurd to me.

The system is broken. No sense in enforcing responsibility. I have had to fly out for depositions for trial on foreclosures, which turned out to be attorney groups that specialize in trying to get homes free to folks based on a technicality. We got a positive judgment at this trial with a foreclosure sale date, but they filed yet another motion to overturn it. I just keep on working, since thinking about it drives me nuts. The group fighting us had some young cheese-ball attorney just pulling down billable hours and nothing else, in my opinion, for his client. I would sit there thinking, poor guy, must have finished last in his law class and had to go to work for street sleaze. In the deposition, there was a debate about my driver's license, the lawyer wanted to review my date of birth and address. What the heck did that have to do with his guy not wanting to pay his mortgage? Was he impressed that I looked so good for someone my age, was he interested in me? Wow, you folks as taxpayers deal with some of these court costs! The young pup wanted to know where I worked prior to the loan industry, since this was obviously pertinent to his guy, our borrower, not paying his mortgage. It just dragged on with inane questions that skirted the real issues. Part of their strategy is to wear us down so we cry uncle, btw (which is 'by the way' for the non-texters) I don't cry uncle. I look them in the eyes and they can see me thinking, *screw you!* My lawyers can confirm that with you if you like.

We even had a debate about the fact I pay for insurance on the house. Why? This guy hasn't paid in years; and the insurance had to be paid. Well, on this one deposition, as I alluded before, it was one of those cheesy law firms that either took a monthly payment or got a cut of the principle and interest reduction and then made wild promises to the borrower. These court cases are all about billable hours and cash for the law offices, not about justice or saving homes. BS money-making scams. These attorneys make money dragging it out in the system. Damn billable hours, but it cost us a few thousand for the trips, which is charged against the loan and would be charged to the borrower in the end. We know in these cases, they will never reinstate, they just trash the home, live it in for years for free, we end up not only paying the insurance, but the taxes, and other expenses, and then get it back when it looks like crap.

Any reason coming to mind about why you might think I am not fond of these Super Lawyers? These guys know these people are in the wrong. They know they will lose the home in the end, but they get hundreds upon hundreds of folks paying their firms mortgage money in exchange for representation and at the end of the day, the legal rep will say they are sorry, they have done all they could do, good luck and get out of their offices before the next sucker is coming in.

Sure, maybe one in a thousand is getting the screws put to them by a lender, that is only a tenth of a 1% and we are not part of that percentage. We give these folks an opportunity to work a deal. The final chapter is that some folks just cannot afford a home or should have never received a loan in the first place, face it, this is reality and they need to move on and deal with it. There is no right in this country to own a home or a car, or anything else, regardless of the interpretation from the Government, Captain America, or your neighborhood mouth piece who just hates anyone making more money than him.

In October 2010 the headlines were ripe with stories about "ROBO" signers (*mindless drones signing documents without reading them*) in mortgage companies just rubber stamping documents and affidavits and going to court for a sale. In our case, we are so small; we have to read each loan file numerous times, so that is not a problem with us. But in the end, what is the real story? Ok, these large firms are out of control and maybe the T's haven't all been crossed, but people haven't paid their mortgage regardless of the technicalities. It is my personal opinion that if you borrow money, you have a contractual right and a moral right to pay it back. Pay up or get out. Better yet, call your lender back and try and work a deal. They don't have to work with you, but give it a shot. Maybe they will be like us and try and work a better deal. If not, buck up and make a change in your life and move on.

You were happy the day you took their money, so don't begrudge them when it is time to give it back. A deal is a deal.

TAXES AND INSURANCE THAT MAKE YOU SAY, HUH?

Riddle me this, Joker. How is it that you can have a loan for 3-4 years, pay the taxes and insurance yourself (*this is called a non-escrow account where the lender does not make the payments for you*) and then when I call to let you know that your County has sent us a delinquent tax notice and your local agent has cancelled your homeowners insurance, you say, *"What? I thought it was in my mortgage payment to you guys?"* I-D-I-O-T. These folks either are dumb or are playing stupid. Usually they play dumb for a reason to feign surprise or whatever that oh no, you mean you weren't paying our taxes and insurance. Either way, it is appalling. It is like the borrowers who know they gambled and need to deal with it, at least those folks you can work with. For an escrow account, your loan docs tell you whether you are escrow and if taxes and insurance are included, and if you don't really know, please just ask. But to have years go by and you actually write physical checks to the county tax office and then voila, you claim you had no clue you should do it every year, only tells me that yes, you are just lying, which doesn't go over well at all.

We had a borrower get angry with me since her loan had an escrow account, and a portion of her mortgage payment, was going to taxes and insurance like most loans in America. She didn't like this and said she wasn't a slave and she could manage this on her own and she didn't want her loan set up that way. Ok…if you say so. We did as she asked and guess what? Yep, the house is now in the process of foreclosure and taxes are not being paid. Give me a break. So it seems she did really need someone to manage her money since she couldn't do it. It is just a never ending story. Some people are never ever happy and it is always someone else's fault. Does that ring a bell right now in politics?

Ok, how about the borrower who owes $6,500 in taxes with a tax sale coming up? This borrower understood they were in foreclosure; they haven't paid us in over 26 months and hadn't responded to letters, emails or calls for those two years. I even knocked on the door and also had a contractor try and get their attention with no luck. Then, 30 days prior to the tax sale they call me and plead, *"Can you help us out please?"* Say what!! I asked her what she wanted me to do. Of course she wanted me to pay her taxes. No kidding. No, not kidding, she wanted us to write a check to the tax office to pay her delinquent taxes when we had been trying all year to get her attention and start paying the mortgage. Another one of those Not only No but, Oh Hell No! Moments.

You don't pay us for two years and when the local government is coming to take your house away, you call me to pay your taxes for you. This was far out! Well, the reality is I was probably going to pay the county the day before the tax sale. I told her I didn't plan on paying it this week or next, sorry, and why should I help her when she hasn't paid us in 2 years? Why should I help when my calls, letters, and attempts to contact her offering reduced agreements are ignored? Those questions were met with silence. We paid the taxes for years, carry the insurance on the property, and pay our bank monthly for the interest on the money backing the house and they have the balls to call me for help. That's the trend and expectation in this country, hand out and palm up.

The Government wants us, small business and everyone else to give up our money, our time and basically destroy our business base for the good of their constituents (such as these awesome borrowers), however, they are not prevented from taking a home in exchange for Government debt. Believe me, if you owe the Government, they WILL come-a-knocking with cuffs. We hand over everything on a silver platter to help keep these folks in their home, but don't you dare miss a Government payment, those guys will pull the carpet out from under you on tax sale day unless you come up with the cash. No excuses. Don't you dare short the Government or cause them to layoff Government employees.

You cannot make your mortgage? Oh, then the lender should lower your payments and forgive significant value on the home and readjust it and take the cash loss right in the behind!. You owe the government money for taxes? Say what? You worthless taxpayer, you need to pay us now or get out, ridiculous, we cannot forgive the taxes or lower them, on your knees slave and worship at the altar that is your Government. YOU SHALL COME UP WITH THE

MONEY OR YOU SHALL BE SOLD INTO TAX SLAVERY.

But, don't worry; you can shortchange Middle America, just not the Government, oh no. All bets off when that happens. But we will end up paying the taxes and waiting until the foreclosure sale and they will call us again pleading to stay in the home for nothing. Huh?

Note: On this situation the borrower eventually paid the taxes days before and my check was returned from the County. Turns out they had the cash? Account is still in foreclosure and we are waiting for that home to sell. Now, where did the borrower come up with almost $7,000K in such a short time when they cannot pay a $1,000 mortgage? Huh?

We eventually took this home in foreclosure and sold it. Didn't make any money but got it off our books.

LIVING LARGE!

Another borrower we worked with for 3 years was always delinquent with well over half the payments not received. I cut the forbearance deal with the warranty deed and kept on them about the lack of insurance on the property, the delinquent taxes etc. I was tired of getting nothing and paying everything and decided to record the deed and evict them. I ran a new title search and these folks managed to gain over $60,000 in new liens on the property in 9 months. You have to really work at it to owe people that much in such a short amount of time, and that didn't include the $40,000 they were behind with us. I had to foreclose on them to erase the liens. They also called and asked me to help since it seems 3 generations lived in this sweet house, with a pool, fountain, marble touches, and a 3 car garage. I also found out they owned three restaurants in the Houston area. So now I get it, we were helping them finance their restaurant business. Give me a break.

I had someone do a drive by and in addition to the home; they had some sweet rides in the drive as does everyone else. How come everyone has a BMW but me? I did a personal drive by in 2011, and saw two BMW's in the driveway. Wait a minute, I cannot afford that. How do you do that and not pay the mortgage? They buy a huge home, luxury cars and then whine to us? Close one of the restaurants, sell it, pay us off and go on your merry way. Quit leaning on us. Before you know it, the American taxpayer will bail them out. Yep, regular taxpayers trying to figure out how to get Bobby new cleats for football or how to put tires on the car, but their hard earned cash will go to delinquents like this.

So they tell me they have generations of families in this large home and they can afford the pool, fountain, nice cars, but not the mortgage? They filed BK right before sale day as this seems to be the logical thing to do. Must have seen a legal billboard on the highway….SAVE YOUR HOME, LET US FILE BANKRUPTCY FOR YOU, EASY PAYMENT TERMS. Huh? We are waiting on foreclosure at this point. At least it was in Texas and Texas kicks butt over other states in making people honor their obligations. If they ever secede from the union, I am moving to Texas and defending their sovereign right to exist. Onward Texas!!

As a note, we do finally own this property and the old owner called to thank me for my patience. Say what? My patience? It wasn't planned, believe me. The courts wouldn't let me kick you out earlier. I couldn't say much. My patience? It was forced patience. One year of charity rent to them. I don't own three restaurants. My friend suggested I go eat at their restaurant, ring up a large bill and then walk out on the bill. When they stop me, just say, how does it feel? Funny thing about this is that you can go to jail for bailing on a restaurant bill as theft but not bailing on a mortgage payment in the hundreds of thousands. Yea, that's fair.

SICK, DYING OR DEAD, WHAT'S YOUR EXCUSE?

Of course I love the borrowers who seem to have constant medical emergencies and miraculous recoveries every few months. I got one message about one surviving with a brother where *they had an 8% chance of living over death and that week they couldn't walk*, but previously they were supposedly stripping for money and the messages go on and on. What the heck did that have to do with paying us? I am not sure I understood the whole brother's medical and death disaster on this one.

This renter was a previous borrower and I got some message many moons ago about her having to be in Hawaii for 2 months and not having money to pay the rent? That was a new one. *Hey, I am vacationing in Hawaii and haven't worked in a while. I will pay you some rent when I get back, although I am months behind and will never catch up!* Maybe she needed to hook up with our delinquent borrower jet setting around Europe? Who knows what these people are thinking?

I think this message got scrambled in-between; we still let them stay in the house, months behind in the mortgage and then months behind in the rent. Are you seeing a trend with some folks here? People do live pay check to pay check and they never choose the home. Vacations, cars, toys get priority on payment.

How about the borrower who told us their daughter had a stent put in that ran from the brain to the stomach? Say what? Is that even possible and why would you do that. This is also the borrower who had to "get away" to "get back in touch with herself" and that is what she used the refinance cash-out for…how about 'get in touch' with what is right and touching your checkbook for us? Come on people. You had to burn $30,000 to go find yourself and get your head straight? You watch too many movies. Wake your lazy butt up, go to the mirror and whoa, there you are, yep right there you delinquent deadbeat. I am just tired of hearing these folks talk. It is an injustice to those really in need, those who have serious problems and want to keep their house and want to do it the right way.

How about the borrower whose significant other went down after *getting hit by meat*? Excuse me, did you say meat? I still laugh at this one. She tries hard as she can, I think, in working with us and is a breath of fresh air, but I always wanted to know. Did someone have a meat fight with him? Did half a cow land on him? Did he slip on steak? Nope, she didn't elaborate, it was that he just got hit by meat and left it at that. Dead silence after she told me he got hit by meat, not a description of how it happened. Bam just got hit by meat. I didn't want to pry, but folks usually finish a story. Maybe by the time I get this book done I will know the whole story and they and I will laugh about it. They are still struggling and months behind, but I won't pull the trigger for a while as long as they keep trying, but eventually the chime will ring and I will have to do something I probably don't want to do. But I am sure there is some reasonably sad story, but on the surface it is quite funny to recount. Come on, it is funny at this point. Hit by meat! As of today, I have a close business acquaintance working hard to help them fix credit and find a refinance. They have done an excellent job of trying to get back on path. I wish the best for them and to duck when they see meat flying next time.

There are those people who have to spend thousands upon thousands on a funeral for a relative and then want us to forgive months of missed payments, because when you bring up that you had to pay for a funeral for a family member, everyone seems to think, ahhh, how sad, and I am supposed to forgive the payments. I am past that now.

The point always seems to be loss. When you ask us to do these things, do they realize it ends up with our families paying the bill? We have flesh and blood behind these homes and the lack of payments hits us directly, not some faceless entity that some Americans think should just absorb loss after loss on their behalf.

Faced with losing the home my children live in or giving someone a nice casket and catered funeral is not a tough trade off. I go with the home for the living. Good people with tough choices at times, but you have to make the smart decision. I understand some folks just have that heart to sacrifice and they are usually the only member of the family that steps up to the plate, shame on the others who don't help them.

I have a young couple who stepped up to the plate and pay for funerals for the grandparents, no one helped them and they got behind. They, however stay in touch and catch up with their obligations. I have no sympathy or respect for other family members who allow them to make this personal financial sacrifice on their own. They tell me, no one else even lifted a finger to help financially, which is sad, but kudos to them for still paying their debt. This young couple has done this twice now, but they keep plugging away. I actually have the husband working for us on rehabilitations in hopes he can earn some money and buy the home back someday. We can only hope!

At this point, we say, protect your homestead. Face it, we have no clue what really happens after our loved ones are gone, but I would hope they come back like Patrick Swayze in that movie Ghost and find a way to slap the stupid out of people for making poor financial decisions. Honor your family and friends in prayer and through the message of how you spend the rest of your life, not by buying a golden casket and putting your homestead at risk.

Then we have the folks with whom we provide a new agreement, along with our brand of financial counseling. We inform them this is short term, but they still resort to financial stupidly? One I am thinking of at this moment was already chastised previously (um, see Disclaimer). I informed them that they needed to try and make some changes to help themselves, they seem receptive, but then they go out and spend tons of cash on something fun, or a stupid so called investment, or get caught up in a scam for sending money to Nigeria. You may laugh, but those scams exist because people fall for them. They actually send money to get money. I know! We work with some of those people. Either they are lying and are trying to convince me they are stupid, or they are stupid, no other explanation can exist. Sure desperate people do dumb desperate things, but c'mon, think think think about what you are doing before you do it. There is no easy money to be had folks, ya'll jacked that up by defaulting on millions of dollars in loans.

People will never cease to amaze me. Although we have good people out there who know who they are, we have too many who just don't get it. But again, this was a high risk portfolio, so it is full of those with poor financial discipline, poorer financial choices and even poorer use of most resources they get their hands on. What can you say? I guess you figure they are numb to collections agents, nonchalant and clueless when it comes to not paying their debt, expecting some bailout eventually will come their way, so why should they change their ways? They always seem to survive, always seem to have a home, take a vacation, or have a nice car. Debt? What is debt? Pay someone back? Nah, not necessary, since they continue to get credit, continue to have people sell them material things all day long. Why should they change their habits, since they are living the high life. It surely needs to come to a screeching halt. But when it does, do they end up protesting about the inequities of wealth and they want theirs? Yea, sure they do.

As usual, something will happen to intervene in their lives and save the day for them. That something is the money that 53% of us pay to the federal government, that money they think is rightfully theirs. If this doesn't happen, they resort to calling Captain Justice League America Lawyer and start crying about losing their home, their car, anything and everything and that the lender is a big bad man and can you save my home and Captain starts calling you a bad man and wanting you to give the folks their home for free or at a greatly reduced rate. Then the leader of the free world goes on TV and blames the banks, corporations, anyone and everyone he can and people follow suit and start to believe, yea, it is their fault, not mine. Give me a break. Then the cycle starts all over again.

I'M FROM THE GOVERNMENT AND I'M HERE TO HELP…?

In 1986, President Ronald Reagan said the nine most terrifying words in the English language are 'I'm from the Government and I'm here to help.' I always thought that was funny, but now I see so much of that is true.

I say the Government is one of the most terrifying things in the country. Prior to getting into this business I wasn't really enamored with Government, and prior to that I worked in Government and wow, it showed me how incompetent Government can be and then witnessing the mess it was creating during my time in this business, I had no other doubts about it. Yep, they could be a waste of breath and resources in our Nation's capital.

Consider this. Politicians, whether it is the President, Senators, Congressmen, etc., spend time in Washington and leave with Government pensions and in the President's case, round the clock babysitting and "God" handling. In my opinion most of them don't have a clue as to what we minions go through, no matter what they say. They are coddled and most assuredly get accustomed to this sort of handling and notoriety. If someone were to break into an investment home the President or some politician owned, they would lock the guy away for years and you won't see the President being chastised as some villain for wanting the house back and the trash taken out. It wouldn't take him $8,000 and months to remove a bunch of dirty drug punks and people who trash what they think is now their home. Nope you better believe those bums would be out the door in no time and would be paying for it in many ways. In our case, we paid!

I think it is odd that politicians can occupy their days creating new legislation on a daily basis. When is enough really enough? A nation of laws is a concept that I understand, but why is there a race to make new laws on a daily basis? Yes, there is a race. Regulations continue to grow like wild fires. politicians resumes are full of their accomplishments, and those accomplishments are usually tied to what legislation they wrote or co-wrote. Wow, let's clog up the books with more laws or entitlement programs. Continue to strip us little guys of freedom and our money. They make us work harder to keep what we earn and they find more ways to give it away to someone else.

Let's not debate the clean air and clean water issue, are how bad the corporations are in this country, when in reality we have the greatest way of life and some of the cleanest water in the world and surely some of the most efficient and cleanest manufacturing in the world, bar none. It seems it is the minority groups that dictate our policies now. Just like in the housing industry where we are throwing enormous resources for the few who make deliberate decisions with their finances.

Some environmental group wants to cripple a company that wants to build a factory on some desolate piece of property and they will come in and say Lewis and Clark may have stopped to urinate there, so we must safeguard it. You stand there in the weeds and blowing cold wind with nary a person around or evidence of human life anywhere and you scratch your head and say, what the heck?

Groups restricting people using open lands to recreate with four wheelers, motorized vehicles? Let's restrict everything we do for the benefit of this small group. I say to them, get out of the way. Go build your vacation home in ANWR, or even take your vacation there in the cold blowing tundra, because that is your baby. The ANWR debate is laughable, but again a small group of people end up throwing up roadblocks.

How about focusing on those folks trying to do damage to this Country? Oh, *we can't do that,* you say? This would mean tapping their phone to find out if they plan on blowing up Times Square. Oh, we have to read them their rights right after they kill many of us, and if we don't read them their rights, well, the fact they admitted they want to kill the infidels cannot be used in court. Say what? Some bonehead tries to kill my family and then admits that he wanted too, well I hope you aren't around trying to play compassionate buffoon with some free lawyer and give him comfort, because you might get in the way and get hurt. You want to make sure they are treated humanely in jail; maybe they were on food stamps while here or unemployment and social security benefits perhaps. Let's give them free homes, let's forgive their debt to other people. Yes, let's give them OTHER PEOPLE'S MONEY. Just for the heck of it.

Yea, focus on taking care of those that know how to work the system, steal our future, and gather wealth that is not rightfully theirs. Yep, that is Washington's job, to even the playing field by taking from the ones that bust sweat and tears and give it to the ones who have their palms out so much they need sun block on them. DC's resume of laws and legislation is their badge of honor. Badge of honor my butt. In the twisted Washington DC world, it is backwards. How about a resume showing where you have reduced laws and burdens on the citizens and businesses. No, in the Government mindset, we need to give to those who don't give a damn or who cannot manage their finances, or who are here illegally. It is OTHER PEOPLE'S MONEY! (Remember OPM) What is fair should correlate to what is reasonable. Listen, there are people who possibly just smoked dope during high school or just didn't care and didn't take the path others did, which was to work hard, possibly college, or break strides to success. So is it fair everyone should be entitled to the same rewards based on past behavior? I am thinking that if I watch the news enough I will see some of our borrowers and renters at the occupy Wall Street type events. Nothing but a big party to them.

I was angry when I wrote this part, watching the national debt climb and climb and our politicians smiling and waving everywhere they went in private fuel sucking jets, day in and day out on the campaign trail, stumping for more lawyers, politicians and we end up picking up the tab while we scrounge and hope to take a weekend off somewhere. Hard to respect these folks for how they run their own lives and this great Country.

I remember a few years ago a piece on the local news about a couple in dire straits, retired and losing their home. They showed a picture of them together, looking so distraught and you surely felt bad. Then you read the story. I am not exact on the numbers, but they had a home for over 40 years where it was paid off and then they decided they wanted a boat, so they take out a new loan on the house and then have a mortgage, then they do it again for a new car, then a vacation, then more luxury items and before you know it they have a debt on the house close to $300K and they couldn't make the mortgage in their retirement years. This seems typical of people in financial distress. Here you have a couple going into their later years with a paid off home and now they go to the media and government asking for some assistance after years having fun, buying items to play and now we are to feel bad for them and reach for our pocket books. I say turn around and go figure this out yourself and don't look to me for help. This is a great country that rewards hard work and when you decide to make these sorts of decisions, well guess what should happen? This should now be YOUR problem and not mine.

Yes, we are a great Country, a Country that takes care of people pretty well already. I do think that what this country needs are more parents who care about what their child is doing in school and not expecting teachers and others to babysit their offspring. Maybe they would grow up with a sense of responsibility to hold their own and the sense to know that success and yes money usually comes from hard work. We need more people who instill a work ethic into their children, people who know where their children are at night, know who they are with, and people not expecting the Government or even their neighbors to keep an eye on them all the time. We need people who understand they need to pay their debts and not look to the Government time and time again to bail them out.   We need people who care about pulling their weight.

We spend an enormous amount of time trying to find and create legislative excuses for people. Of course there are people who are in great need and have come to a spot in their lives not through their own doing. There are programs out there in abundance to support these people, but when is it enough? Do we destroy an entire nation to save a few? No. You cannot save the world. Wasn't it Spock of Star Trek fame who said it best with this quote? "The needs of the many outweigh the needs of the few." That Spock was a brilliant Vulcan. I would bet his ship was not in foreclosure. Over 95% of people are paying their mortgage, people that are strapped down and watching their finances. Sometimes you have to let the system work out the chaff. How do the folks feel that are pinching pennies and then watch in the news about how we are trying to bend over backwards for folks who over extended themselves, and then scream for compassion and fairness? Really, you need compassion or do you need counseling in financial discipline. Quit spending beyond your means!

We have a Country striving with people trying to find their own specific recognition either through their financial distress, their religion, their race, their culture, their sex. We are a Nation of cultures and races, sure be proud, but be American first. I tire of this quest to only identify yourself by your economic status, sex, religion, race, culture, some odd affiliation, or whatever. We have enough class warfare in this country and people making money off it, we have race-baiters and enough people trying to make a name and money for themselves by ensuring Government keeps broad separation between the ethnicity, religions and cultures of folks. Let's get back to the melting pot; we all bleed red don't we? Well, maybe not in DC, what color is undisciplined spending blood look like anyways.

MORE GOVERNMENT RHETORIC

During my time in the loan business there were many programs that came out of Government claiming to save the housing industry. Initially, we paid close attention, actually the Government officials paid attention, as I was asking people 24/7 to pay their debt. These legislative officials were all analyzing the potential for programs set up for homeowners (weatherizing, insulating, and other such plans). Eventually we tired of watching and waiting for the next program idea and realized everyone was on their own and the Government never had anything that truly worked. It was all party streamers and speeches and that only provided a pat on the back for those guys.

We then thought that hey, maybe Fannie and Freddie could relieve the burden on banks and us by buying these loans and then giving the folks what they wanted: Low low low or no loan interest and forgiveness. That would have been much cheaper than the trillions of dollars they were spending buying the confidence of their biggest voting blocks, the unions or whomever. Let's just let this fall out on its own, and actually, why not? Everyone got themselves into this mess and they need to find a way out on their own.

Politicians tend to spend their time helping out the two percent of the Country and not the Country as a whole. The thing our Government leaders seem to have is either ignorance or massive compassion for the mistakes people make. Financial compassion is a piece of cake; especially if you are given the keys to a money chest that is filled with the hard earn blood and sweat of your fellow citizens. You don't feel the pain yourself but you get the pleasure of people kissing your butt for giving them money (*OPM folks*!!). There are programs aimed at people who have no clue (except for the honest few). They don't know how to manage their finances, and those who do manage their finances are expected to spend their dollars to bail the others out. And that my friend leaves a pretty bad taste in the mouths of millions and millions in this Country. Washington has put a lot of pressure on the wrong people. They want folks like us to write off debt, lower principle amounts and just flat out give people our money in the name of what, compassion? No, this was all about looking good in DC. As far as I am concerned, these politicians, and those who support them, could have pooled their money and bought those loans in foreclosure, offered those wonderful terms they wanted, and forgiven whatever amount they desired. Right....it is one thing to tell others to do it, and yet another to put your money where your mouth is. Politicians don't put their money where their mouth is, they take money, and they give other people's money to support their causes. They seem to enjoy sucking money from us little people.

At times I laugh when watching some serious reporter interviewing someone who claims they are losing their home and the bank is not cutting them any slack. In my opinion, regardless of what you think of banks, they are backed by OTHER PEOPLE'S MONEY and you have no right whatsoever to ask for your home free and clear, or to expect a break just because you plead and provide whatever reason.

The next thing is something I learned early on. Look past the teary eyes and sad stories and look into the loan file, the person's finances and usually you find they were not good stewards of their own money. Yes, some people have true hard luck stories, but we cannot afford that either. If you think we should forgive debt issues based on the intensity of a story, then there wouldn't be any foreclosures in this country, since everyone that listened would run to their door and offer to pay their mortgage. Now, I have yet to hear that happen. Maybe it has, but it isn't on the news and this is what they want our families to do. How fair is that?

Sure, there are people that just had a bad break, illness, etc., and that is indeed sad. However, this book deals with the other large group that spends, does whatever they want and when the road comes to an end, the puppy dog (or Puss n Boots) eyes come out, the hand turns up and they beg for money and a second, third, fourth chance. Far more often than not, the Government rides in with a black limousine and hands out our money and some reporter is standing next to them, offering them a shoulder to cry on.

I used to laugh at the internet jokes about just sending everyone in America $100,000 or more in lieu of these massive bailouts. Now it makes more sense.

But, with politicians that doesn't happen. You have to punish the people with money, the people who spend wisely, and tell them to give up the future financial health of their children to bail out that lady who blew thousands to go find herself, the couple with two too many cars, the ones who think we should finance their child's private school and over-priced shoes... just because. Let's see, we can spend billions to bail out union folks, with heavy benefit plans, or bail out Government workers, where, in a time of job loss for the private sector, the Government sector grows larger. Go figure. The Government is not there to help the vast majority of folks who work hard and need the money they are making to raise their children and support their families.

The Government is not there for the people who forego the new car, because why support the logical consumer, who knows it doesn't make sense to buy a new car when they are struggling to pay their mortgage? No it seems the Government is there to help squatters and tweekers stay in a home that is not theirs. It is there to allow people who have a life of running away from debt, and this behavior will continue so long as the Government offers them a financial mat to fall back on.

Now, all you folks who hate the man or woman who make money don't go on about your definition of justice as some sort of socialist or communist model of economics. I don't want to hear it.

There was one legal case that nearly killed me (hypothetically speaking) involving the Pennsylvania County. The case required we have conciliation conferences with the borrowers during the foreclosure process. Initially I thought this was a good idea; sure, let's make people talk to me that had been ignoring me historically. After time, I learned to hate these conferences. They were nothing more than a delay on what was inevitable foreclosure. You keep threatening to take away a child's toy to make them comply, but then just give them more, what makes you think they will behave the next time? Heck, they want more toys!

These conferences only delayed the foreclosure process, and cost us enormous sums of money due to the fact the home was a free rental opportunity during this delay, these folks never intended to make it right and we had to pay for the legal expenses of this debacle. It did create more Government jobs with the highly important need for a housing counselor. Ha, seriously, ha!

The couple in this case owed us $26,000 to fully reinstate the loan and make it current. They didn't have any cash as a good faith option during this mediation type conference; we were supposed to be all-forgiving while they bring nothing to the table. What had they been doing with their mortgage money for the 12 months they hadn't been paying us? It's a trend which has been brought up before. These folks had jobs, so where does their money go? Seriously, what were you doing with the mortgage money! If you have no money after 1-2-3 years of no overhead costs then you cannot afford that home! Period! The deal they wanted was an interest rate equal to what a good borrower would get, and oh, they wanted us to forgive their debt. Ok, none of this was good with us, of course. We wanted full reinstatement or the house. They ignored my calls, emails and letters for a year and now they wanted the Government to force MY hand? These folks had money to put their child in private school and yet wanted us to subsidize their home. Well, private school is cool, but I could only afford public school for my sons and I produced some quality educated members of society that way, they could do the same and pay their bills at the same time. New cars, private school, and a delinquent mortgage is what they brought to the table. They also applied for a program funded by stimulus money. Yes, your money and mine. (*OPM*)

Here is the deal. If they got approved for the stimulus, which at the time the attorneys said it looked good for them, the Government would pay us the full reinstatement on their behalf and then we have to drop the foreclosure and reinstate the loan. Sounded fine for us, right? Well, here is the kicker. The Government would put a lien on the house for the amount of that second mortgage which equaled the full amount they gave them to reinstate the loan. So check this out. Not only do they have to now pay the full mortgage payment, which they obviously couldn't, or didn't, before, but now they would also have a second mortgage payment against the property. Ok, who in the crowd thinks this is smart business from the Government and for the taxpayer? A few years of free living, no reserve to show for it and now would have two payments? Anyone? Hello? Come on people! What sort of common sense or sound business practice dictates that you fund a second mortgage to people that cannot, and will not, pay the first? What is the Government thinking? I will tell you, The Government is thinking VOTING BASE. Oh, poor baby, have some more money and if you get in trouble AGAIN…we will go through the conciliation process AGAIN. These folks will be in foreclosure bailout number four, then, just come back and do this all AGAIN. Give me a break!

This is a fine example of a couple that needs to be renting an apartment for life. Owning a home is NOT A RIGHT, it is a privilege. Stuff happens, deal with it. The end game here is going to be foreclosure, we will own the house, the Government second will get removed and you the taxpayer just lost more money. Money this couple no doubt spent on the private school tuition, dinner out, vacations, new cars, maybe massages, and who knows, possibly some other weird wasteful stuff!

The bottom line with Government bailout programs for housing is they are a complete failure. The large percentage of borrowers failing in paying their home loans had high interest rates for a good reason. They had a continual history of bad financial decisions, supported by getting more and more money and more and more second chances. Most of the programs required you to be current on your mortgage, and that wasn't the case in most situations.

As I noted before, there are those politicians who wanted judges to arbitrarily reduce the principle owed. This is simply asinine business practice. If you want to dry up credit, give a judge or lawyer the ability to reduce your investment on a whim and no one would lend money in a county that had that law. Who thought of this in the Government? How damaging and idiotic was this determination? Man, this is just idiotic, no explaining it otherwise. As we proved in 2010, we didn't have the stomach to allow banks to fail and people to fail. Why? Politicians want to be your friend so they could continue the largesse in DC and get your vote.

In my time I have worked with some struggling companies and we never got a Federal dime. Here is my message to Government in this housing crisis. Get out of the way. Allow the small percentage to either fail or work their way out of the mess. We offered deals, but with the Government floating overhead, seemingly offering bailouts, people weren't interested in making it right, always hoping for yet another serving of money from above. The industry will clean itself out; homes will get rehabilitated and resold to folks who pay their mortgages. Penalize those that use the system to take advantage of other people's homes, money and compassion. There are thieves out there among us, who only care to get theirs regardless of the cost to you and me. Government, stay out of it!

I NEED HELP!!

What can I say about the loan support industry? I guess I have to start off by discussing the third-party providers (such as realtors, brokers, loan services, contractors, etc.) surrounding the loan companies which actually lend money. Some are good, some not so good. Companies that get large tend to emulate the Government, with wheels losing air, cheap gas, and they start to sputter. Some of our early third party support vendors tended to be like the government. This is where people start to gauge their day with not how much they get done, but by the clock on the wall wondering when they'll get their next break or when it is time to drive home. Clients, and priorities, then get lost in the broad scope of daily drudgery.

Let me tell you, some of the most dishonest and lazy people are working under the pretense of providing support to people and they think they know everything. Throw in the fact that virtually anyone can get into the real estate business and you have a conglomeration of loons, boneheads, stupidity, and ignorant selfish hogs. There is the occasional good guy or lady who had an ability to make money and be honest at the same time, but this is a rare concept to most in the industry.

A friend of mine, who is an agent and who I routinely gave a ration of crap about his business, once said in frustration that he wished it was harder to make it as an agent and that the fees should be much higher to keep more people out and present more barriers to the people that swarmed to the career. Let's take a count of hands of everyone who has a relative, friend, etc., who is a real estate agent, how about broker? OK, put your hands down. How about those who know a nuclear scientist? No one!! Come on, rocket scientist? Again, no one. Chemical Engineer? No one! Come on, let's see some hands.

Are we surprised that with the rash of easy college degrees our children chase nowadays and then they have difficulty in finding a solid career that doesn't require a technical degree or even business degree?

During my initial months as the keeper of all hats with this loan business, I had contact with our loan servicer, who was local to the State of our corporate office, which at times was and continues to be an upstairs bedroom in my home. This group handled the inflow of payments, late notices, foreclosure coordination, you name it, all the organizational b.s. that comes with a loan portfolio and they charge you out the butt for it. It has nothing to do with success, in fact the worse the situation, the more money they make. Quite the business model!

Don't dare call a borrower, get personal and cut a deal to help them out! That creates a rift in the cosmos and relationship stream flowing through the loan servicer. You see, many a loan servicer doesn't want the borrower talking direct to the lender to work a deal. It is better for them to have their drone try and do it. A person who doesn't have the authority from me, and who couldn't get any job other than in a call center to talk to the borrower about his loan and what he thinks the lender would do. In October of 2010, we saw news reports of firms suing big lenders for having no-name drones sign foreclosure paperwork when they never reviewed it or knew nothing of the loan. It doesn't surprise me one bit. There are good servicers and there are bad ones.

These were our issues with this particular servicer. Horrible service, absolutely horrible, and their lack of loan knowledge was not good for us, as the lender, or for our borrowers. The hesitation in allowing us to talk direct to our borrowers was treated like a Federal offense. We determined the issue of us getting between the servicer and the borrower was our way to provide direct honest communication, and which was frowned upon. How can you make all those fees if you cannot con people and loan companies that they need the mindless drones that they employed? As time went by, I came to understand why. I always wondered if they told untruths to other borrowers, who were with other lenders that didn't pay attention to the details like we did. Maybe giving them false hope and driving a wedge between their lender and the borrower. It became hard to tell where the truth was coming from, borrower or servicer. Were they giving false hope of loan modifications where there was no way we would approve such actions? Were they telling people it was OK to skip payments since a new plan was on the way? Hmm, maybe, but they chased them anyway without our direction or approval in hopes of nailing a fee. In retrospect firing this servicer and hiring a new one was our best business decision at the time and probably one of all time for the business. Great people to work with and those we could trust.

Anyhow, this first servicer was full of drones that were incompetent, people that didn't care since it was our money and who could not make a good decision or speak honestly and openly about our loan portfolio, these folks were just plain ignorant as one of our family team members noted on occasion. I tend to think their actions were a result of management telling them to push the fee items and as a result we got poor service. You have folks trying to make a few dimes and who do they listen to? They listen to management driving revenue. Oh well, they were long gone after a while. Yep, not all corporations are great, but over time they fix it or go under. Not like the government. I still choose corporate America or Government in America any day of the year.

Sorry about the use of stupid or ignorant, pretty blunt and to the point, but we tended to use this term often after working some time with these folks. Our team likes other descriptive words such as dim, thick, dense, slow, brainless, but let's just stick with "stupid is as stupid does." To this day I claim our best support from our first stupid servicer was *after* we fired them and they seemed afraid we might cause *them* damage. Yes, we wanted to sue them daily, but there were a couple of good eggs there that helped us straighten out the messed up assignments and title issues, and for that I am very thankful. As for suing people, one member of our team wanted to sue virtually everyone we came in contact with that screwed up and that was often. I cannot really blame him, and we ended up suing a few folks, but we settled or gave up, since it is only the attorney who benefits through a lawsuit.

Thankfully we eventually found some good counsel to support us, good lawyer is an oxymoron, and they are few and far between. But we do have some good decent counsel at this point. Good guys you can talk too who aren't always focused on billable hours.

The final straw with our first loan servicer was when they didn't agree that we couldn't offer what was called a forbearance agreement. This type of agreement reduces the payment for a year and carries the unpaid interest on the loan. Now, check this out. This was our money, our borrowers and our decision and we thought this was a great idea to keep folks paying and keep them current for a year, allow them to relax and recover, and spend some time trying to clear up their credit. Sadly, as you have realized from the gist of this book, most just took it as a cut in mortgage with some new cash available and didn't spend much time trying to fix their situation, but we tried. Even worse was the loan servicer, these folks wouldn't support us or the borrower with this type of agreement. Why? Well, you need to realize they made money on each loan modification and that is what they wanted to do; permanent modifications and then swallow that large fee without water.

Did this tee us off? Of course it did!! But what we offered seemed simple, give the borrowers a break, let them get their finances in order and maybe get a refinance elsewhere, since we made it clear we were a small shop that didn't modify loans and give new loans. We didn't want our money tied up for 30 years. As private investors, we wanted out as clean and quickly as possible. It was our hope to offer a break in the action, a time to allow borrowers to gather their wits and focus on fixing their financial situation. In retrospect that was a pipe dream.

This was already starting to be a mess with the Government getting so involved and with damaging legislation that was being discussed about forced principle reductions and other damaging ideas to the industry. People hear this on the news and they get more focused in not working a deal or making a payment. It gives them hope that some miracle is coming so it is like chipping concrete with your hands in working a deal. Not going to happen. The forced principle reduction never came about due to some clearer heads realizing this would ruin the lending of money on homes in the United States. Bad idea which some politician came up with which would have effectively destroyed the loan industry. Every one now gasp in surprise.

As for our new plan to help people out, well, we had a big formal meeting, much like the Government when you have too many people in the room who think they know everything and have power; all the while neither is correct. We were told at this BIG meeting that this had too much, wait for it….*Headline Risk.*   *What?* They explained that this might cause some bad press. Still I didn't get it, this is something our borrowers wanted, something other people wouldn't do, and they were worried about what?   I swore I could see my partners' veins about burst and was waiting for the Khrushchev shoe incident to be replayed in that conference room.   We had just went over their severe lack of support in calling, getting payments to us, overcharging and duplicate charges for fees, horrible monitoring of foreclosures, mistakes, and they had no logical responses.   This worry over headlines was the last straw.   We scoured the internet for options, almost used a young man who we foreclosed on in California for this support, almost purchased the software for me to run the business, which I was so excited about I could pee….right?   NOT!

We stumbled on our new servicer and we have never been happier.   They had humans that listened to us, humans that could think, humans that once they understood our business approach and strategies and options, they could relay that to borrowers without a problem.   How refreshing.   They actually believed they worked for us and not us for them and they certainly didn't work against us or the borrower.   Ok, did I overdue making my point here?

MORE SO-CALLED 'HELP'

We also had a short life experience with a firm that handled the sale of our properties after foreclosure. What a waste of time. These folks are basically real estate agents with a software program. They call themselves REO brokers. Or Real Estate Owned Brokers. They are everywhere. Agents who couldn't sell a home and just bought a database so they could overcharge lenders for foreclosed property disposition.

These folks were nothing special. They had locks changed and quotes for repair service. It was just a network of real estate agents who wanted a quick sale and who got their buddies to give them inflated quotes to repair the properties before sale. You couldn't ask questions, no, don't you dare question the quotes for work. I tired of this quickly and immediately cut ties with them and handled this myself. They are known as "REO" companies. Run away fast when you see them coming.

People always had an interesting time dealing with us. They would Google our names to make sure we were real. I would at times send over my resume and a bio on the other officer, just to get people to talk to me. They couldn't find an iota of information on me, but they always found background on him and then would call back and work with me. We were small, a two bedroom corporation that had corporate meetings at Costco, since we loved that $1.50 lunch deal, kosher dog and coke. Great dog! Hey, we got our version of a conference room with food and drink readily available. No one ever knew we were discussing a $20M + business at a red and white plastic Costco table and this worked for us just fine. But really, $20M in this business is rather small, very small.

Now real estate agents are up next on the list. Whoa. Getting a good agent is like trying to find an honest lawyer. Yes, it is that tough, no joke! I cannot tell you how many times I was told I couldn't do something or sell something for that price and it seemed they were always wrong. I spent some months with a Florida agent or broker, not sure what he was called. We tried to put our business out there in Florida together with this guy. He was attached to us for the sole purpose of making a killing, which is understandable I guess in retrospect now that I understand agents and how easy it is to become one. Now becoming a good real estate agent is a totally different ball game folks.

At the time, we had visions of expanding, working with Fannie Mae or Freddie Mac (yea right) and getting homes and loans from banks and helping them manage the home and eventually turning these things over for some good money. Yes, we had visions of sugar plums dancing in our heads. Ok, so it didn't quite work out. This guy promised the world to me. He stated he could do anything, handle any property, clean it up, etc. It took me a few months but I found out he was a nice guy, but we considered him a little whacko and he really didn't follow through on those promises. I remember meeting him at a local mall when he was on the way up to his mountain condo with his girlfriend. One of the first comments he made to me was, "Check out my girlfriend, isn't she hot? She used to work with Christy Brinkley." Ok, yeah, it is very cool to have a hot wife or girlfriend; I have one, yes just one folks! My boss has one, my sons seem to always have them, but damn, to make that comment isn't what I call appropriate the first time you meet a potential business associate, especially when you hope to start trusting each other and making some money it is a bit odd. I didn't know his short little Napoleonic butt from Adam, and I wasn't real concerned about how HOT his girlfriend was. For you women, you would be glad to know she dumped him and he was so smitten, he went into some downward voodoo spiral for a while. He actually disappeared for a week and I couldn't get results on evictions etc. he just disappeared without a word. We fired him that week, but I actually hope he is doing well in whatever he is doing. Yep, he broke up with his girl and went off the deep end. He went to see a palm reader or something like that, got into yoga, voodoo healers, and who knows what other foo-foo business he got himself into. Used to tell me about his overly active dating habits while stoned and such, hey, great call buddy, call me again sometime.

The business stuff that worried me started with him wanting me to dump our first property in Jacksonville at $40,000. He told me straight out I wouldn't get more than that, even after rehab. He told me hookers were on the street and other shady stuff going on around the home. I said "No way!" I had it repaired and put it on the market. I had to redo most of what he called his "great contractor's rehab work" prior to the sale. Still grates me at times. I sold this home for $115,000 a few months later with about $10,000 of rehab work. I actually visited this property and it was sweet, nice quiet neighborhood and not a hooker in sight. It must have been her day off. Hmm...do you think maybe he was trying to get someone (a friend) to buy it for $40,000 and then fix it themselves to sell?

Yep, baby, they were trying to scam us, imagine that, a scam artist in this industry, say it isn't so! We had the same situation on another property where they told me to just scrape it and sell the land and he could probably get me $15,000 for it. One month later, after rehab, it was valued around $125,000 in a down market. Yep, more bums in real estate scamming us again believe it or not. We ended up renting it at $850 a month after $15,000 of rehab work went into it, and eventually sold it for profit.

I came to learn overall that most people claiming they were there to help, they were not to be relied upon. They all wanted you to sell quick and cheap so they could get a quick commission. This guy worked it though. He needed work and wasn't used to getting dirt under his nails. Always trying to get me to invest in some project, like a large empty condo project, or buy his condo at a "cheap" price, maybe a beach nightclub that was "killing it" or invest in some other ventures that celebrities were into it on the Florida scene. Of course, all of these were "guaranteed big winners." I always thought, *go ahead and do it yourself; if it's so great, good luck, and make some bank.*

The tough part of using agents is when the house needed some work. Some had "great contractors" that they used who gave us outrageous quotes. In Connecticut, for example, the agent told me the basements of two homes had flooded and needed the area chewed up, pumps put in, etc., to the tune of over $40,000 each. We wondered what happened to the homes over the previous 20-years without all this work. I asked the agent to check the gutters and she told me they were fine. I ended up sending a man up there (yes, lack of faith in what I was being told) and, guess what? Yep, he found both houses had the gutters ripped off and one had a French drain installed upside down, so all the water drained against the foundation and leaked into the house. We fixed both issues for considerably less than quoted and fired that agent. This was an agent who had actually claimed she visited the properties and checked them out. I got a sobbing email about how they were a leading real estate agent in that area and they were sorry they didn't meet my standards but wanted another crack. Screw them! Why is that that every agent is seemingly "a leading seller in their market?" I swear every ad I see says that. I guess in today's society everyone gets a soccer trophy and nobody loses, and everyone is a leader in their market. So sweet, I guess they wouldn't admit that they suck and are the worst? Always watch agents who say they work with someone you can trust. Right! I had better luck getting contractors from the web or places like Service Magic. (Thanks Peter – oh, see Disclaimer!)

I have to say I ended up finding a guy in Las Vegas we liked at least for a while, that is until he got a little weird with us and was holding funds, not responding for weeks on end. God, even the good ones go bad. We just didn't have many homes there. We also found a guy in Pennsylvania who was great to work with. We worked as much as we could through these guys and used their experience to help us find agents in other parts of the country. These guys vetted agents in other states for us and help us find property managers. They helped us evaluate property pricing and virtually anything else they could pass on that was helpful. They tended to be honest and we would discuss the market, economic conditions, you name it. They seemed to have a strong grasp of real estate and would give us honest feedback and they both had a great sense of humor. These guys were straightforward, found us great pricing on rehab when we needed it and I think they understood that long term relationships were based on honesty and integrity. They had it, most didn't.

Now, if you are in the market for a property manager, be very very careful. I say it much like Elmer fudd did. Try it. But instead of saying you are hunting rabbits; say you are hunting property managers. It is, much like dipping a hand in a basket of vipers. You are not sure if you come out with a bite or a snake, usually all snakes. Find a good one and hold on. I gave three houses to manage in Florida to one manager. We had just finished rehab, putting in new appliances, blinds on all the windows and paid for cleanup through them. Amazingly enough I start to get calls from tenants about the house being a mess, appliances old and rusty and when I asked, were their blinds on the windows, they said what? So here I had an agent/property manager who not only took my money for non-existent cleanings, but also stole all the appliances and even stole the blinds from the units. They eventually gave me my fees back and wanted us to walk away from each other. Thieves. Just can't trust people anymore. Too sad.

I think in 2011 the Government finally understood that all those borrowers who couldn't make payments and who were given a new loan, still had the consistent habit of not paying a lower mortgage payment. I think the failure rate was over 90% on those given modifications on their loans. But thank God the administration wanted to use all our money and our children's money to keep giving these folks a break and help the situation. Hey, Washington D.C! Wake up! I have said this before. The fact is some people simply CANNOT AFFORD A HOME and that is why they make apartments!

OXYMORON: LEGAL HELP

Lawyers! Ok, what can I say about lawyers that I haven't already said? The good ones go on to bigger and better things while the bottom-feeders start working foreclosures for our borrowers while advertising on freeway signs. Lucky me to work with the bottom-feeders. Now, let me say that overall I have good feelings about some of our current counsel. Maybe I just have had a run of back circumstances. They are not all bad. Some lawyers weren't dropped on their heads as babies and could actually work without making constant mistakes. What we came to find out while being with our first servicer, was that all our foreclosures were put with legal foreclosures mills right out of the chute. Big mistake. These are large firms that handle foreclosures like big box retailers sell toilet paper and actually the box stores service is worth much more than these legal mills. By the time this ever gets to print, there will be considerable press about certain law offices in Florida that will be dismantled. I understand that one of these firms' owners has one of the most beautiful homes on the Florida coast. Paid for by guys like us and they even include it on coastal tours. Now that must be a home. I wonder if it is now in foreclosure. Those folks really screwed the pooch, but this particular lawyer made a mint. Before he crashed and burned, we pulled all our foreclosures with that firm and placed them with other small firms. Easy to call and reach out and touch the attorney when they are smaller. If you can, always find the hard working small attorney. I can vouch for that.

In the summer 2010 some of the legal firms we had used were making the newspapers and not in a good way, but by then we had already decided to cut them loose or wean ourselves from these LARGE FORECLOSURE MILLS, since they are wholly ineffective. As a foreclosure mill, it means the firm will do mass amounts of loan foreclosures and work them like cattle to slaughter. It just seemed like they always put the cattle in backwards. They would miss dates, would foreclose in the wrong name or just screw it up in some other simple manner. You had to stay on top of them and they tried to make you feel like you were bothering them. Forgotten documents, you name it, they blew it. It was too a point that I had to put ticklers in the calendar file for every stage in the process and to keep on them about moving forward. I did this for one particularly horrible foreclosure mill in Florida and one in Pennsylvania on a weekly basis. It would remind them of what they needed in order to proceed with a foreclosure and eviction. If you didn't stay on top of them, they just floated in space without someone intervening to push the issues. How big banks put up with this, I just can't imagine. Big banks must get their butts kicked on delays and missed opportunities.

When we moved servicers, we had moved virtually all our foreclosures to smaller firms for some personal assistance. We made much more progress, at a much smoother pace and we were much more efficient with our dollars. It just makes sense to do business with someone you can sit across a dinner table with and discuss problematic issues and get them resolved between you without going through a mass of clerks and drones who just flip folders and papers without much in the way of results.

As usual some attorney's office makes a huge mistake that we end up paying for. One attorney fought us tooth and nail on a missed sheriff's sale due to their offices error. You would think they would stand up and put their money where their mouth was and make it right. Ha! I had all the emails about asking if everything was ok, bid instructions were there and asking if EVERYTHING was in place to proceed with the sale. The answer I received was "yes, *everything was a go*". Not so quick it seems. The day of the foreclosure sale of this $500,000 home came and went. The borrower never made payment one on the house and was in the house 2 years. Yes, two years without a payment. This borrower was gainfully employed but county records showed he screwed everyone with nonpayment, I guess we were not that special. It seems our attorney, although they told us all was well about 5 times prior to the sale date, forgot to send papers to the sheriff for the sale. They told us initially it was our fault and that we didn't provide bid instructions. To this day, I remember sitting at the airport and my partner yelling into his cell phone at the attorney and asking how they were going to make this right. They eventually admitted their error, when they saw the string of communications between us and them. Simple truth was that they just dropped the ball. When it came to the finale of this event, where the rubber met the road, this firm didn't make it right as they promised. But don't be surprised. In our business we pass on the names of the good attorneys and yes, pass on the names of the lousy ones. Goes to show you that many law firms are not about honesty, they knew they screwed the pooch. Not much we could do. We were small peanuts to this firm, so their reputation with us didn't matter much. None. None at all. We end up paying the price for holding this property for another year and carry that $500K.

I did have one good experience with what many considered a foreclosure mill. A new partner joined the legal firm we were working with and chose our little case to assess the workload and get his feet wet. He did a bang up job on our trial with no history in this business on his portfolio. I sometimes laugh about the fact that we had attorneys on both side of this case that were probably making more in a month that the house issue was worth. He had no real preparation time and nailed it. Problem is he was a new partner and there would be no second chance on the next case, it was a one-time deal for us. So we were back to the pens to paper to pick a lawyer from the masses in their firm, but the guy we worked with was so much better it wasn't even a fair comparison. Thanks to this one lawyer joining the firm, we were considering moving files back to them as they come up. It pays to be competent and when they made an error he wrote a check and mailed it to me. You just don't see that sort of commitment to excellence anymore in this country. I can respect that.

On to the title companies, uh oh! I think they hire from the same pool of people that servicers, real estate companies, legal firms and anyone in line to support the loan industry choose from. We had a title mistake soon as I got on board and it took months to straighten out. There is title insurance for a reason, but what the heck, don't ever try and use it. Like trying to wash black off coal, it won't happen easily folks. It is always someone else's mistake. Where are the people in this country who believe in a sense of fairness when they screw up? Fix it and make it right, don't make people sue you to make it right, ridiculous. Title companies are a waste of time. I get more errors on title reports that I can verify through contacting local counties. Just not reliable at all. Best of luck to using one. It just becomes a natural thing to pay the title charges. They want the money now, but when it comes time to fix things, you can never get someone on the phone with the authority to fix a title error.

I sure learned more about people in this industry than I ever imagined. More than I wanted to know. The bottom line is this, regardless of Government oversight, where 1/3 of them are off on any single day, regulations, better business bureau reports, nonprofit support and other groups related to real estate to oversee or provide support are there to overlook the industry, the industry runs amuck with people just looking to make a buck.

The last word on third-party providers, get references, check them out, sit down with them, understand what they want, what their goals are, Google© them, find out as much about them as you can, before you head down that road as business partners. But of course this is true for everything in life. Understand what and who you are going into business with. Same if you are a borrower. Take time to understand what you are signing up for. Don't just look at the dollars they will give you. Eventually you will have to pay the piper and claiming ignorance or stupidity is just getting tiresome to listen too. Please understand the relationship and the consequences of actions or inactions.

AT THE END OF THE DAY

Each day that I work on our portfolio seems to always bring some strong emotional issues and misconceptions with our borrowers and even more so with our renters on foreclosed homes. You continue to hear in the news about how horrible we LENDERS are, and how we arbitrarily kick people out of homes. We are painted with broad strokes as villains. This painting of business folks like villains seems to be nothing more than a political strategy from folks who don't have a clue about business. And it seems they don't have much of a clue about politics either.

What most people don't hear is that we are just normal working people trying to earn a living and fighting everyday against the same issues as every else. We have medical issues, we have finance issues, work wears us out and we do react to these emotional pleas that come on a daily basis. But that doesn't make for good print news.

Let's look at what I consider the facts. The vast, and let me emphasize, the VAST majority of people in foreclosure that are offered modifications end up right back in foreclosure. This is a sad fact. It is going to happen. I heard a financial analyst on the evening report, Charles Payne I believe, said this whole thing *was like trying to catch a falling safe.* It is going to hit and going to hit hard, with no safety net to stop it. He was right on. The Government was really trying to do something that was impossible with all these borrowers. His comment was in reference to the over

$20 Billion spent on the Home Affordable Modification Program (HAMP), a do-it-yourself loan modification program to supposedly help homeowners which failed miserably. He also commented that the Government would have been better off to just mail a check to these borrowers to pay off the loans. He was so right. Government is so inefficient and most of that cash was lost in the bureaucratic process. Let the natural flow of loans happen and move on.

Personal experience showed me that many folks saw a reduction in their mortgage and they got excited and then reacted with incurring more debt. When they see a plan to get relieved of a mortgage amount and have an opportunity to receive some cash the natural tendency is to either play with it or save it. The problem is that many people tend to be horrible with financial discipline in their lives and they tend to just go out and spend that extra cash almost immediately. That being said, some will no doubt think, *"Hell, I got forbearance this time, so why not miss a few new payments and beg and borrow for yet another chance, blah blah blah."* These are people that treat this as a green light to go buy that new material item or get another high interest loan for additional cash to spend on some extravagance, like that trip to Maui or to get in touch with their inner idiot.

This drives me close to insanity, and as I move forward I notice the stress building inside me from listening to this every day and having to tell people that enough is enough and wanting to scream bloody murder at them. I worry that they are breeding and instilling this sort of financial lack of discipline on their children. Our future foreclosure borrowers or entitlement class are right around the corner. Maybe this failure in the mortgage business is an exercise to teach our children about personal responsibility. God save our country...please!!

Folks, it never stops! The calls and the complaining continue. The calls from people telling me that they had to bail out a relative, friend, other family, you name it instead of paying their mortgage. Then they think we should forgive that amount or ignore the missed payment, really folks? You want us to finance your relative's problems. Is that what is happening, you take the money you owe us and fulfill what is their obligation instead of your own, is this what we are to believe? Pure and simple, it is b.s..

As an example, we have a renter who was originally one of our borrowers and over a year behind in payments. We worked a deed-in-lieu deal on the home and took ownership of the house. We worked a deal so he could stay in the house and became a renter, same sad story. However, this time I had previously met him and his little boy. He was a very beautiful little boy. He seemed so innocent and just wanting a place to play with the family. You walk away a little different, but you have to keep your perspective; unfortunately, we cannot save the world, or every cute child we run across. Parents make choices in their life that affect their children. I ultimately cut his cost of living under a roof by 40% and took on the insurance and taxes in order to give him at least a year of stability. Within eight months he was over five months behind and currently we have asked him to move. We can no longer provide free housing. Just not acceptable for us when we are trying to survive and maintain a property, the insurance and taxes and be expected to keep a roof over their heads. This is just not going to happen.

When I finally got people into this house, it seems he had made more rooms and sectioned off the house for renters. Great? Now we have to rebuild it back to code. Another landlord making money off our backs and not paying us. Happens more times that people think.

Where will they go? I don't know, but they found a place already, which makes me believe they had the means all along for housing but took advantage of our generosity. My friends now understand why I am losing my compassion for people when they hear these stories. We just get taken advantage of. Currently the government is mimicking this and allowing a whole segment of society to do the same to the government, which in turns means you and me.

Maybe someday we will tire of working this way. Emotionally it is hard to see this little boy move, but we are running out of patience. It costs us money to keep these homes, our money, not monopoly money, real hard cash. So everyone that thinks we should just give these homes away or forgive all the debt, let me say one more time, *we also have to pay our bills, our debts to the counties, our agents and property managers and our families.* I knew early on that is was inevitable that we will eventually be working to move him out and getting someone in place that can pay on a consistent basis. I just didn't want it to happen soon, but it needed to be done.

We are what many see as the *big bad lender*, but we are letting someone stay in a house for over two years without most of that time being paid for!! Part of his rationale for not paying his mortgage and then rent was that he gave money to the Haiti relief fund. Did he really? No. He gave (OPM) OUR money to the Haiti relief fund. If they want to demonstrate this sort of compassion and assistance to people, then they cannot unilaterally decide to take their mortgage (our money) or rent (our money) and give it to someone else, or some cause, and then claim they helped others and then ask us to forgive their debt. No, that is not how charity works. Charity is from the heart, giving from yourself, your wallet, not deciding for us, hey, the property owner won't mind if I send his money overseas right? No, pay your mortgage or rent and then take some of your expendable funds and donate that to the group or people of your choice. This is what responsible people do. This is what I do.

It is a fallacy that they used their funds to have contributed to these efforts. Taking money out of our pockets to finance their charity of preference is wrong. But this is a continuing trend with my calls. Someone had to help someone else out. Would you really give your mortgage money to someone else and then hope you don't lose your home and put your child out on the street? That is so crazy. I gave to the Haiti relief efforts out of my own pocket. Now, I don't want to hear that I was more financially qualified to give and that is not a fair comparison. Folks, you don't give away money you don't have or that is not yours. If you do this, then prepare to suffer the consequences of eviction and live with it. No tears, so sob story. This planet has disasters all the time and Americans give more generously than any other Nation, but they give of themselves. Before you buy that new car, new high tech device, or give overseas or send money to relatives, ask yourself what it will do to your family. Do you have this sort of expendable income or is this just a WANT that you have to have! Don't assume the people you owe money too will say, ok, sure, take what you owe me and give it to someone else, spend on a luxury so you can get a pat on the back and then turn around and call the lender, which is me, names of disgust for asking for free rent or free mortgage and then I say no.

We all want to save the world in some fashion, but we cannot operate like the Government in trying to save everyone. You just cannot give away other people's money. Are you listening on the Hill? This behavior tears me up. I am at the point of telling folks they are making a conscience decision to lose their home, and I do tell them this, day in and day out.

I am so tired of hearing people say they got scammed, or they had to help out a sister or maybe help out a mother and father and now they want us to forgive their debt. It just doesn't play anymore. There are so many options out there for people in trouble and that need help. Don't assume we are the first charity to call. Don't pay others with money meant for your home, the structure that keeps a roof over your head. You start making those decisions and you have to live by them. When your lender is a small group of families and you don't pay them but put money elsewhere, you have to understand that we may not be able to survive your charity and decide to take the home to liquidate. It is a business at the end of the day, it has to be, and it's a lose-lose for the borrower and their initial 'good intention.'

As cliché as it sounds, you all know what does roll downhill? Right, you got it. We have debts to pay and expect our borrowers and renters to pay their debts so we can pay ours. Survival of the fittest is going on every day in this economy and we strive to be one that survives. We have doled out compassion and forgiveness in barrels folks, we can't do it anymore.

Sometimes the people you help are just a part of the undisciplined financial class and you need to quit helping. Maybe you need to pull that crutch away from them and let them stand on their own two feet. It is a great possibility that they need to let these folks around them fail before they get the message to start taking care of their issues instead. There are costs behind those homes, insurance costs, tax costs, you name it, but somehow our Country tells people that it is ok to direct other people's money to their pet cause and then whine, cry, and bitch when we don't fund those independent choices.

Amazingly enough, you can actually go on-line and get an enormous amount of information from folks telling you how and why you should <u>not</u> pay your mortgage. What is that about? A section of society devoted to helping people skirt their financial responsibilities. It just makes me slump in my chair in disgust. Much of the information is in error or misguided, but it is like some game to many people. *See how long you can stay for free and the justice system supports it.* Who gets hurt? No one you think? Think again and then pay attention about why it is so hard to get money nowadays to purchase a home. The whole country suffers, and yes, it does keep rolling downhill folks.

I look forward to the end of this business, if not for the ending of the stress, but for the simple fact that there is a severe amount of cash strapped to the large number of borrowers and renters deciding to forego rent or mortgage payments. They make decisions and choose to do other things with these payments. Let me tell you that I got tired of asking the team to write personal checks to cover the costs of these homes and rentals. This isn't fair for our borrowers who busted their butt and dealt with their own problems in life whether medically or financially. I learned to despise the folks who would say the mortgage or rent being a month late is *no big deal*, the same people cry that we don't have compassion or don't care about their situation. I care. I care that you don't care about our situation.

We are the last ones you think about after you make sure you go out, take a vacation, give money to family and friends, make sure your Hummer, Mercedes, BMW is covered, lose money to gambling, scams, making sure you have the latest model phone and you data plan and text plan is open, you name it and then turn to us to somehow forgive your debt which we didn't cause. By your actions you caused this. Crying doesn't change things. People make independent choices in life that lead to all these foreclosures.

The family that chose to pay more for private school than they had to pay in a mortgage and then ask us to forgive the mortgage until the child graduated from high school. Yea, another big set of steel (*you know what*) there. That is nothing but absurd! I understand the desire, but you again made an independent choice to spend that mortgage money on private school and whine that we want our payments. It is amazing how this farce exists in this Country with people who want and want more, and then expect someone else to pay. The justice system perpetuates this habit by protecting these people and that simply drives up costs for those who make their payments. Borrowers wouldn't allow me to manage their finances or give financial advice, heaven forbid, but they want me involved to forgive their poor choices or concede to giving the money to a cause or family/friend.

I am not saying we are destitute, nor do we need to be in order to ask for payment on these obligations. However, I continue to actively look for jobs to work in tandem with this business in order to relieve some pressure on the team, and to get my mind off the constant depressing stories about these homes. It is hard to have extended bouts of compassion in this business.

There are some borrowers and renters who just never seem to have a good day. The people who I trusted and then turn on me for the second time or third time like, the guy who gave me the house out of bankruptcy, I cut him a cut-rate deal to rent it back with an option to repurchase. You would think he would be thankful. He wasn't. He probably laughed when I paid off his liens and then had to sell the house. Scum that is all he was to me at this point. I will never forget that he paid me for one month and disappeared without communications. Calls, emails and letters go unanswered until the day he gets the legal eviction notice and then tells me that his wife was sick. Does this explain not picking up the phone or returning a call for 2 months? No it does not. People still take care of business during times of duress, especially when we are speaking about the roof over our head. He called to give me yet another issue. He couldn't drive the certified check over because he needed new tires on his car. He never had a check ready, just a weak excuse. Can't tell you home many times money orders or checks get lost going to our mail address. Just amazing that the post office seems to have difficulty with just our address. Come on folks, you can do better than that with your stories. I am ashamed that I fell for so many excuses because I wanted to believe these people needed help. But I had to stop and I had to tell them, *NO MORE*.

No more telling me your medical problems, car problems, spouse problems or your problems with your children. It is not my issue. I do not need to be burdened to help you figure this out. I cannot run your life for you, nor do I desire to run it for you.

We have done our part, lost many dollars, given many breaks. Help yourself. Give us a break, I am done, fried. Start paying your bills or move in with family members, better yourself, change vocations or maybe email some liberal talking head, some Cadillac liberal and ask them for a handout.

There is so much money out there for education to improve yourself, so get off your potato chip eating butt and move forward. Right feet, left foot, then repeat. But you have to be willing to put down the beer, get your ass off the couch, put in time after work at a local college, or get a trade, just do something!

FALLEN ON HARD TIMES

I have a limited source of these folks that truly understand the result of their actions. I have one borrower with excellent retirement income. He pulls in over $6,000 per month, so many of you out there will not feel sorry for him no doubt. Federal retirement income. Yep Federal retired employee. Feds can make some bank that is for sure. Anyhow, every so often we are close to taking the deed based on a prior agreement, but I hate to do it in this case. I continue to send e-mails to him, leave messages about them taking the initiative in selling the home and making a change in their lives. I have done everything I can think of to help him, cutting his payment for 2 years, putting him in touch with credit repair. You have heard me say this before. Nothing sticks. I call, write, call again and write again. I am only met with dead silence. Silence! Yes silence, because everyone knows that if you ignore something long enough, it goes away, right? Sure it does.

The borrower took a refinance for a significant amount of cash out of the house in order pay for the medical costs his daughter incurred in an ATV accident and she wasn't on insurance on her job by choice. This is the story that was related to me direct from the borrower. Seems his daughter declined to accept insurance with her employer. I read through the lines that she wanted to spend this cash on some luxury and not insurance premiums since young people are pretty much immortal. Yes, she was young and invincible or so he insinuated. He needed money to get her back on her feet, literally. We had a long talk and in the end, my last question to the borrower, *"Was it worth it to lose your home so your daughter can be healed and walk again?"* He responded yes, and then we agreed we could move forward and if the end result was he lost his home, it was going to be OK since he had come to terms with it. I am not sure how this one will turn out to be honest with you. They have some healthy liens they have also incurred on the property so they will end up in a bind, but the house does have equity and let me tell you, it is a sweet custom home. Don't feel too sorry for them. As of this writing they are still a few months down, but I have hope they will come to their senses and eventually fix their finances and refinance or sell the home and get us out of the mix, or so I hope.

I eventually had to start foreclosure on this one to get the borrower to call me, email me back, pay attention and boy, did he. He called me about 10 times in few days. I was busy so I let him sweat and eventually gave him an earful. My offer to him is a deed in lieu option with caveats. I will give him 18 month lease with repurchase. He claims he needs much less to buy it back at what he owes us. I have agreed to pay for credit repair and consulting on negotiating away and paying his IRS lien to our satisfaction, so the lien can be removed. I have yet to get the documents back signed to initiate this deal. We shall see. Closing in on owing us $700K.

We can never financially forgive or overlook these financial decisions people make. It is their decision to make and they cannot expect us to bankroll these decisions.

I have a few borrowers with spouses or close family that have gone downhill due to illness or accidents and they are trying valiantly to catch up. It is hard to apply the pressure on those folks. Some are sending in chunks of money at a time, which is held in trust by our servicer. This feels like you are at a game and rooting for them to win, so we can win also. Sometimes the emails and messages are just hilarious, but in a good way, since they let their emotions and feelings run rampant and tell you how they are going to make it. It is not to mock, but just the positive exuberance they expose in saying, *"Dang it, I am going to make it."* You hope those people do make it and I point them to the credit repair places and brokers in hopes of them getting a new loan with a "real money lender". Some will succeed. When they do succeed, that is a good thing for everyone involved. Many will not succeed and it's emotionally damaging for everyone to experience that, but I also have to protect the assets of the families that I work for and who have entrusted me to manage this investment. I always tell myself that we cannot save the world and think about the families in our group and how hard they work to prop up this investment. Priority one is not letting them down. Life can be selfish, but that is the nature of things. You work for yourself, your family, whatever gets you up in the morning to earn some dollars. And true to form selfish needs can collide. My need to keep this investment above water and your need to have me forget your payment is due. Oil and water folks, they just don't blend well.

THE ENTITLEMENT GROUP

This is my favorite group of borrowers. This is probably also a favorite of my fellow hard working Americans. This is the group that always expects someone to bail them out, always! Some of these folks called right after the election in 2008 as I noted earlier by asking for that *"Obama money"* (referencing the Government surplus and/or earmarked stimulus funds). This request sure caught me off guard. I was thinking, *Wow, people really think that the President will pay their mortgage?*

I was guessing these were the same people that were expecting someone, like us, to come up with cash or forgive their debt. They used their money from everything from vacations to clear their head, to the extra cars, luxuries you name it. One thing they didn't use it on was the house it seems. I saw firsthand when I visited properties. Care and tending to the HOME was not a priority for these people. They may love their home, but it sure didn't show. But this is our fault America. We coddle these people with giveaways. Politicians basically buy them off with our money so they stay in their voting base, promoting poor financial behavior. They think it is too painful to cut them off of the Government faucet. Listen folks, there are hundreds of worthwhile programs that our Government funds, not so sure that it should be in the tens of thousands.

Building an entitlement society is not the goal I think we need to set our sights on. I think the news in 2010,

2011 and 2012 is showing how dangerous it is to a State's economy when you continue to create legislative giveaways to certain parts of the public. Free housing, free medical and the list can go on and on. What incentive do the masses have to cut themselves free of entitlement? They don't have the incentive to cut themselves off. But look at who pays for it, you and I pay for it! Oh sorry, to you people that think the Government doesn't take money from me, your neighbor, family and friends for those bailouts and checks you get, go back into your hole and keep thinking that there is this Government money tree out there and it is unlimited.

The truth be told, too many people think that the government does get money from trees and how dangerous is that. And they vote nonetheless. Good lord people, education is available everywhere. Maybe you can consider turning the channel occasionally, since you won't get all your knowledge from court TV, regardless of how smart the TV judges seem.

FINANCIALLY DISABLED

This group of borrowers has some of the entitlement group in them, but overall they have no idea how to budget and save. When you look at their finances, they spend like a child in a candy store with credit cards and their credit report shows pages upon pages of delinquent accounts. If they cannot pay with one credit card anymore, well let's just find another one to buy with, rack it up. This is long term. This is not just months into a job loss like they might want to convince you. The teacher that takes the summer vacation and claims she cannot pay her mortgage because she has been out of town for two- three months. The odd pause in my conversation with this person stemmed from my knowing right then that she felt she shouldn't pay anything during your summer months off. Just weird. A teacher? Say it isn't so! And no doubt she is teaching someone else's children this same message.

How about that borrower who was finding herself for months in Hawaii and couldn't pay the mortgage because she spent too much on her trip? Hold it; I know what you are thinking. *Did people really tell you these things?* Yes, they did. I never said many were brilliant, did I? Again, who would even tell their lender those lames excuses? Well, at least some of the stories, if true, are amazing when you think they told me, their lender, and the real skinny behind deciding to not pay their mortgage or rent.

Well the people who are in this group are also in line of the *stupid* group. Sounded good in their heads and made sense, so why not use it as an excuse. They do live among us.

How about the borrowers on their third or fourth foreclosure bailout? Say what? Yes, they too exist. They just go from one financial disaster to the next. As I noted in a previous chapter, a borrower actually told me she had to take out an eleven percent (11%+) loan on the house so she could get back in touch with herself after divorce and take a long vacation. Come on man, give me a break. I wonder who around her thought that was smart. I will remember to remind her to take the box of vacation photos to her next living situation to remind her what that vacation really cost her in terms of living arrangements. *(We now rent this house out!)* Of course this lady ended up lying through her teeth and playing the emotional card, using her children as an excuse, to avoid responsibility and eviction and it worked on me for a short period of time. I do want to believe and do want to help. I played along, trying to work with her and in retrospect I lost many months hoping that the deal she wanted and which I gave her would work out. NOT! She played me. Our plan was to initially believe these folks, see if we could get them on track to becoming performing borrowers. *Stupid is as stupid does*! But, no more.

We end up trying to do everything the media, the Government and public supposedly wanted done, the problem is, it starts with the borrower in my opinion, not the lender. I can call, email and suggest options until I am blue in the face. But if these folks don't want to accept responsibility, the result is always the same. Most folks and yes, MOST folks want something from us we cannot give. The home free, forgiveness of thousands and thousands of dollars. At this point, I am tired and frustrated and I say to them; *"Just give me the house and get out."* They are so engrained with this attitude of spending for what they want, entitlement, rather than what they need, that they sabotage the rest of their lives and it dominoes right down the road to all aspects of their existence. Again, this is not our problem anymore, give me the house. These folks will continue to have financial problems forever, job or no job, bailout of no bailout, house or no house. It will manifest itself again with some other item or subject. They won't wake up the next day more financially astute and think they should honor financial obligations. It is a disease in our society that is seemingly spreading. They will spend everything they have every month until they are dead and gone, leaving the debt to family/friends, and us.

PLAIN STUPIDITY

Ok, granted, no one wants to ever be called stupid, ignorant or dumb. Never! Heck, I have been called a few choice names more than once and many times I asked for it. But let's face it folks, we have people in this Country that do live, work and walk among us that make you do a double take in the intelligence department. They are not a specific gender, religion, race, culture or geographic location. They all comb their hair different; have different hobbies and different accents. I guess they have one thing in common. They use their freedom to vote for the guy who they think is going to give them the most and could care less about the rest of the Country mainly because they just don't know better or do, and they understand who will GIVE THEM THE MOST for nothing. Politicians come on TV saying what they will give us over and over again and we fall in line, slobbering and waiting for that give back, that free money, food, and housing, just pick some entitlement. If you say you'll give it away, they will come. If they think for sure it is free, they will come running!

These are the people who say to us or in court that *someone fooled them*, or they got *taken advantage* of, or just say they *didn't know*. Now, some of these folks are just cons or escapees from the other groups I described. They know what the agreements in front of them state, and they signed every last one of them regardless of the repercussions.

In our portfolio of loans there is a letter from each borrower that discusses in their own hand writing what they are doing and why. They all state that they can afford the increase in payment. This was smart on the original lenders part, but these people still claim they don't remember writing it or reading, even with the 10+ signature pages and documents that contain the new mortgage payment. All I can do is shake my head in utter disgust. If they are truly in dire straits and just wanted the money to party or buy another item or take that trip to Belize, then admit it, tell me and we will move forward. I will shift you back to the financially undisciplined group and determine what I am going to do with you. More often than not, this involves you losing the home. Since you are either financially disabled or truly not educated in finances, and in that case, a rental is your best option in life, but only if they don't run a credit report on you and deny you housing. Not to worry people. The Government is poised to take more money from hardworking folks and give to those who expect a handout.

REACHING FOR THE STARS

You have got to applaud this group of borrowers. They are the easiest to speak with. They know the game and understand what they did and they know exactly what we are trying to do and don't hold a grudge. Sometimes this could be a small businessman or woman, who now has our money, with their house pledged as collateral. They are banking on being the next Bill Gates with their business venture, but it doesn't always work out. As far as dealing with these folks, I appreciate them the most. Fewer excuses, they even tell me thanks for everything I have tried to do for them, even if in the end they will lose their home. When you sink your dreams and home into business, you better be prepared for the opposite of success and that is failure. It happens.

I have one interesting borrower I spoke to while he was in prison. We would talk during his one phone call per week from the lockup. We ended up agreeing to continue to foreclose on the home to scrub a lien and his wife and children would rent it back from us. Honestly we wouldn't stop the foreclosure at any point with him. Served no *purpose* at the time. He is doing his time and will be released soon. Sure seems like a decent guy. He didn't whine about his confinement at all to me. Interesting story of why he was in prison, but overall, much more decent than folks in the other groups. We will see if he exercises his right that we gave him to buy the home back from us a few months after he gets out of the prison system. His money against the house was used in the liquor business and it seems to be a viable ongoing concern while he is serving his time. Let's hope people are drinking their share in that neighborhood. Maybe not?

In retrospect it is funny that we "negotiated" the situation with no yelling or arguing with calls from the prison. He has offered our team drinks and dinner when he gets out. There is a potential for amusing relationships in this business. The bottom line is that he understood that both of us are making business decisions and business affected his home. He is dealing with it as best he can. I don't even hold a grudge for the short sale cash offers he made while in prison. I just laughed on the phone, saying where was this six-figure money you are offering when your mortgage was due each month. That elicited a laugh back from him. *(I would assume it was spent on the business or family was coming up with cash at this point).*

CLOSING THE DOOR

This business is just tough, with its good days, but mostly bad days. You know it truly sucks when a good day is a day that you get a home back through foreclosure or finally evict a renter or borrower. You get conditioned that someone else's misfortune is something that helps you and others and gives you the ability to move forward. When I am done with this, I am not going back. I wrote this book to have some release, not sure if it would ever get published or have a positive or negative reaction. Ok, I know the answer there, people that want and want and want some more from everyone else will not like the book. Anyone with more than they have is bad, anyone giving them money or assets, is good. Blame society for this attitude, since we as a Nation support this behavior regularly.

Occupy Wall street crowd? What are you thinking out there people? You can't seriously be complaining that you can't get enough free stuff in this capitalistic country. Listen, if you can't get a job with your degree, whose fault is that? Probably yours, more likely you chose to get a degree that was easier and not technical and that gave you a great experience in college without giving a thought about whether you could get a damn job with it. I can't count how many friends kids have decided to choose a degree to follow their dreams. Oh give me a break. Dreams don't pay the rent or put food on the table. Be a parent, buck up and lay it on the line. Get a degree that has a higher degree of success related to it and minor in your

DREAM. Why is it that more foreigners are getting technical degrees in our country and US kids? Ah, but our kids are following their dreams, how cute.

You say you can't stay in your home due to foreclosure, whose fault is that? Stuff happens, bad stuff. Go with it and get back on your feet. Crouching in a park and yelling at people won't work. Makes folks like us even harder in our resolve. The folks that hate business and people who generate jobs and money should be happy. Folks like that have lost millions upon millions of dollars these past few years. We have lost and continue to lose on homes. Where is our justice? Sorry, we don't get any unless we decide to not wash and sleep in a tent in a city park.

What are we to do in this crisis? I say, let it play out. Please please, let the homes wash through the market. Let the foreclosures get processed. Let's get through this hell and get these homes sold to get them rehabilitated. I am adamant, let's get through the foreclosures quicker. Dragging them on for years is fruitless and hurts the industry and hurts the country as a whole. You cannot save the WORLD!! Let it happen and let's move past this. Teams and people do lose; we cannot hand out participation ribbons to everyone in this country!

Let's clean up the housing market this way. Have the Government get out. Get the hell out of the way. Let it happen and let the market adjust. I think folks can see that Government intervention just doesn't work. Governments are good at only a few things, one being waging a war. (*With a good leader that is*.) This isn't a war though, this is about people learning to live within their means and accepting it.

IS THIS THE END

For those that didn't like this book, too bad. My guess is that they never get to this page. We aren't a bad group of people, just people trying to make a living. Too many hurdles in this industry for us to want to continue for any extended length of time, so this will end for us someday in the near future. We just don't have the appetite to build this business, but we do have the acumen to save it. You have to break some eggs sometimes and at this point I will break them and scramble them if necessary.

For those lenders out there and those working in the industry, I say; BEST OF LUCK! I do think things will eventually work out. This country is strong and I would hate to think that we have so many that gave their lives and limbs for the freedom of this country for us to do nothing but bring ourselves down further. If only for those who brought us freedom and liberty we must right this ship and we must buckle down and quit acting like the selfish punks we sometimes are. Nothing is free in life that is for sure, so quit looking for it.

Since this is the 2nd edition, I might as well make some additional comments. I cleaned this one up. Took out the four letter words so as my brother says, it would appeal to a much broader readership. Ha. Not sure about that. For those that know me well, you can interject what you know my emotions are into the correct page, situation, story or whatever.

Since I put together the conglomeration of stories, references and opinion, a lot has happened. We now own over 60% of the assets we had in the loan pool. We are down to performing loans I can count on two hands, but still have way too many loans languishing in the foreclosure courts. Millions of dollars' worth of properties that lawyers on both sides are making money off of, borrowers are living in them free, taxes are piling up Remember that attorneys recommend borrowers don't pay the taxes and insurance, so yes, we pick up that burden. They don't take care of the place and they slowly deteriorate.

But, and it is a but....the end game is with us, we eventually get the home back, albeit years later, albeit in bad shape, but we fix it and rent it or sell it. More often or not we rent it due to the housing crisis.

The ones that hurt the most are the folks who are renting out homes out while in foreclosure and although our loans state this income should by rights come to us when the mortgage is not paid, we seemingly have no rights to enforce this. We still have people trying to cram down principle reductions on us, and while they haven't paid a dime in years.

Our rental business seems to be doing well, but you do get the deadbeats that rotate rental houses, since they play the system. Our houses continually get broken into, A/C systems stolen and occasionally less than honest property managers and contractors.

But overall I have faith. Not in our renters or borrowers but in our business. We are hanging in there. The families occasionally putting additional cash into the system, but I see a light starting to shine at the end of the tunnel. My personal opinion is that a change in government in November 2012 would have an enormous impact on the economy that would roll to the housing sector and we will see greater climbs in value.

As I get better in discerning good support contractors, I save time and money running the business. And as foreclosure finally work towards resolution we can turn a property from a cash eater to a revenue generator with a good tenant.

Faith, you just gotta have faith.

www.ingramcontent.com/pod-product-compliance
Lightning Source LLC
Chambersburg PA
CBHW051449170526
45166CB00001B/173